Modern Switzerland

A Volume in the Comparative Societies Series

Modern Switzerland

A Volume in the Comparative Societies Series

ALDO A. BENINI

California Polytechnic State University
San Luis Obispo

HAROLD R. KERBO, Series Editor

 **McGraw-Hill College**

Boston, Burr Ridge, Il. Dubuque, Iowa Madison,WI
New York San Francisco, St. Louis
Bangkok Bogotá Caracas Lisbon London Madrid Mexico City
Milan New Delhi Seoul Singapore Sydney Taipei Toronto

McGraw-Hill College

A Division of The **McGraw·Hill** Companies

MODERN SWITZERLAND

1 2 3 4 5 6 7 8 9 0 DOC/DOC 9 3 2 1 0 9 8

ISBN 0–07–034427–2

Editorial director: *Phillip A. Butcher*
Senior sponsoring editor: *Sally Constable*
Editorial coordinator: *Amy Smeltzley*
Marketing manager: *Leslie Kraham*
Project manager: *Kimberly D. Hooker*
Production associate: *Debra R. Benson*
Freelance design coordinator: *Laurie J. Entringer*
Compositor: *Shepherd Inc.*
Typeface: *10/12 Palatino*
Printer: *R. R. Donnelley & Sons Company*

Library of Congress Cataloging-in-Publication Data

Benini, Aldo Albert.
    Modern Switzerland : a volume in the comparative societies series
/ Aldo A. Benini.
        p.   cm.
    Includes bibliographical references and index.
    ISBN 0-07-034427-2
    1. Switzerland—Social conditions.   2. Switzerland—Politics and
government.   3. Switzerland—Economic conditions.   I. Title.
HN603.5.B46   1999
306'.09494—dc21   98-14811
http://www.mhhe.com

In one of the early scenes of the movie *Reds*, the US revolutionary journalist John Reed, just back from covering the beginning of World War I, is asked by a roomful of business leaders, "What is this War really about?" John Reed stands, and stops all conversation with a one-word reply—"profits." Today, war between major industrial nations would disrupt profits much more than create money for a military industrial complex. Highly integrated global markets and infrastructures support the daily life of suburban families in Chicago and urban squatter settlements in Bombay. These ties produce a social and economic ecology that transcends political and cultural boundaries.

The world is a very different place than it was for our parents and grandparents. Those rare epic events of world war certainly invaded their everyday lives and futures, but we now find that daily events thousands of miles away, in countries large and small, have a greater impact on North Americans than ever before, with the speed of this impact multiplied many times in recent decades. Our standard of living, jobs, and even prospects of living in a healthy environment have never before been so dependent on outside forces.

Yet, there is much evidence that North Americans have less easy access to good information about the outside world than even a few years ago. Since the end of the Cold War, newspaper and television coverage of events in other countries has dropped dramatically. It is difficult to put much blame on the mass media, however: international news seldom sells any more. There is simply less interest.

It is not surprising, then, that Americans know comparatively little about the outside world. A recent *Los Angeles Times* survey provides a good example: People in eight countries were asked five basic questions about current events of the day. Americans were dead last in their knowledge, trailing people from Canada, Mexico, England, France, Spain, Germany, and Italy.* It is also not surprising that the annual report published by the Swiss World Economic Forum always ranks American executives quite low in their international experience and understanding.

Such ignorance harms American competitiveness in the world economy in many ways. But there is much more. Seymour Martin Lipset put it nicely in one of his recent books: "Those who know only one country know no country" (Lipset 1996: 17). Considerable time spent in a foreign country is one of the best stimulants for a sociological imagination: Studying or doing research in other countries makes us realize how much we really, in fact, have learned about our own society in the

---

*For example, while only 3 percent of Germans missed all five questions, 37 percent of the Americans did (*Los Angeles Times*, March 16, 1994).

process. Seeing other social arrangements, ways of doing things, and foreign perspectives allows for far greater insight to the familiar, our own society. This is also to say that ignorance limits solutions to many of our own serious social problems. How many Americans, for example, are aware that levels of poverty are much lower in all other advanced nations and that the workable government services in those countries keep poverty low? Likewise, how many Americans are aware of alternative means of providing health care and quality education or reducing crime?

We can take heart in the fact that sociology in the United States has become more comparative in recent decades. A comparative approach, of course, was at the heart of classical European sociology during the 1800s. But as sociology was transported from Europe to the United States early in the 20th century, it lost much of this comparative focus. In recent years, sociology journals have published more comparative research. There are large data sets with samples from many countries around the world in research seeking general laws on issues such as the causes of social mobility or political violence, all very much in the tradition of Durkheim. But we also need much more of the old Max Weber: His was a qualitative historical and comparative perspective (Smelser 1976; Ragin and Zaret 1983). Weber's methodology provides a richer understanding of other societies, a greater recognition of the complexity of social, cultural, and historical forces shaping each society. Ahead of this time in many ways, C. Wright Mills was planning a qualitative comparative sociology of world regions just before his death in 1961 (Horowitz 1983: 324). Too few American sociologists have yet to follow in his footsteps.

Following these trends, sociology textbooks in the United States have also become more comparative in content in recent years. And while this tendency must be applauded, it is not enough. Typically there is an example from Japan here, another from Germany there, and so on haphazardly for a few countries in different subject areas as the writer's knowledge of these bits and pieces allows. What we need are the textbook equivalents of a richer Weberian comparative analysis, a qualitative comparative analysis of the social, cultural, and historical forces that have combined to make relatively unique societies around the world. It is this type of comparative material that can best help people in the United States overcome their lack of understanding about other countries and allow them to see their own society with much greater insight.

The Comparative Societies Series, of which this book is a part, has been designed as a small step in filling this need. We have currently selected 12 countries on which to focus: Japan, Thailand, Switzerland, Mexico, Eritrea, Hungary, Germany, China, India, Iran, Brazil, and Russia. We selected these countries as representatives of major world regions and cultures, and each will be examined in separate books written by talented sociologists. All of the basic sociological issues and topics will be covered: Each book will begin with a look at the important historical and geographical forces shaping the society, then turn to basic aspects of social organization and culture. From there each book will proceed to examine the political and economic institutions of the specific country, along with the social stratification, the family, religion, education, and finally urbanization, demography, social problems, and social change.

Although each volume in the Comparative Societies Series is of necessity brief to allow for use as supplementary readings in standard sociology courses, we have tried to assure that this brief coverage provides students with sufficient information to better understand each society, as well as their own. The ideal would be to transport every student to another country for a period of observation and learning. Realizing the unfortunate impracticality of this ideal, we hope to do the next best thing—to at least mentally move these students to a country very different from their own, provide something of the everyday reality of the people in these other countries, and demonstrate how the tools of sociological analysis can help them see these societies as well as their own with much greater understanding.

Harold R. Kerbo
San Luis Obispo, CA
June 1997

Switzerland is a small country. Its surface would have to be extended 227 times in order to fill that of the United States of America, and for every Swiss resident there were roughly 37 Americans living in 1990. On the physical plane, therefore, these two countries do not seem to have much in common. Yet, when we ascend to the higher planes of human existence, Switzerland and the United States have faced a number of similar challenges. On occasion, they have explicitly borrowed ideas from each other, or they have consciously chosen different solutions. For example, the constitution of Massachusetts was the first modern constitution to be adopted by popular ballot, in 1778. When the Swiss created their modern federal state, in 1848, the ideas and experience of the American Revolution was one of the forces shaping the institution of direct democracy. In turn, the Swiss experience inspired the American populist movement, between 1890 and 1920, to introduce instruments of direct legislation by the people in several states and major cities.

The organization of democracy is therefore an area of common ground. The Swiss case is particularly relevant because direct democracy was adopted universally at all levels of government, and American readers, who are exposed to periodic waves of populism demanding more direct government by the people, may want to know how that affects the process and outcome of politics.

But while the political institutions of the two countries, despite major differences, do offer some parallel experience, the question of how to foster the peaceful coexistence and integration of diverse cultures has received radically different answers. The United States has to this day, and with large success, fused its many immigrant groups in the one mold of English language and American culture. Switzerland, sheltering different language groups much older than 20th-century immigration, recognizes four national languages of equal right. The arrangements that the Swiss have created for multilingualism to work are of concern to Americans, particularly with a view of future scenarios that hold English as becoming a minority language in certain regions.

Another motive for studying Switzerland has to do with the demise of ideological alternatives to the free-market economy and the free reign of capital and profit at the end of the Cold War. Switzerland has one of the most highly competitive economies of the world. At the same time, its public sector is strong, in such areas as energy and transportation, and, in the eyes of the Swiss, generally performs well. Also the social welfare state has been vastly expanded in the past 50 years. Switzerland thus presents a mixture of capitalist and socialist institutions that in good part accounts for the prosperity enjoyed by broad sectors of the population. In fact, the Swiss case goes to show that for some purposes "big government" works well.

While the specific Swiss experience in the three areas mentioned—democracy, languages, and the economy—as well as in others may hold useful lessons, or at least valuable points of comparison, also for American readers, it is important to remember at all times that it remains embedded in the culture and social structure of Switzerland. This book attempts to provide this grounding. The principles used in analyzing Swiss culture and social structure are set forth in the introductory chapter, together with the plan of the book. They are kept deliberately simple. If the reader finishes this book understanding some of the inner workings, unique individuality, and, at the same time, the contributions to universal values that this small country has made (beyond the benign irrelevancy of cheese, chocolate, and the Swiss army knife that earned it its traditional fame), then my job has been accomplished.

In writing *Modern Switzerland*, I have been helped by many people who contributed their hospitality and transport, time and expertise, material and access to other informants and institutions, and even computer assistance. I wish to express my deep gratitude to them. They are, in alphabetical order, in Berne: Peter Füglistaler-Wasmer, Edit and Daniel Hunn, Toni Schlaepfer, Dominique Spahn, Elisabeth and Matthias Wehrlin; in Geneva: Anne-Catherine de Perrot and Hanspeter Kriesi; in Lausanne: René Levy; in Portland: Martin Muller and Pia Schneider; in San Luis Obispo: Janet Benini, Willy Gommel, and Richard Kranzdorf; in St. Gallen: Hans Knaus, Hedi Margelisch, and the staff of the Vadiana Library; in Widen: Elisabeth Sailer; in Zurich: Susanna and Dominik Landwehr and Urs Langenegger.

While all of them gave valuable technical assistance, even more important was their continuous encouragement without which this book would not have been finished. My thanks go also to several unnamed workers in offices of the federal administration in Berne who went out of their way to find documentation, as well as to the conductors, coffee vendors, and fellow travelers on the Swiss trains that put up most politely with the author's expansive study on rails. My hope is that the reader will find many images of a society on the move as from a train winding its way through Switzerland.

Aldo A. Benini

CONTENTS

Chapter 3

Basic Institutions   55

Chapter 4

Swiss Politics   70

Chapter 5

Switzerland in the World Economy   98

Chapter 6

Social Problems   116

Introduction

The introduction provokes the reader with the results of a recent international quality-of-living survey. Switzerland received the top overall rating. If it is such an inviting country, what are the fundamentals that account for its unique development? A small number of elementary forces are singled out as recurring themes, and the plan of the book helps the reader anticipate in what institutional fields those forces operate.

THE BEST PLACE TO LIVE?

My parents met shortly after World War II. My father was born to an Italian **immigrant** and a Swiss woman, who spoke German between themselves. In 1946, however, my father was an Italian national, and Italy was painfully recovering from the defeat and destruction in the war. Switzerland had not been involved in hostilities, and life augured well for a young couple. But that was not the way my grandmother saw things. A widow raising six children in a conservative mountain area, her views on the future were firm: "Switzerland has been spared by two world wars. We will be spared by World War III. I do not want my daughter to become the widow of a foreigner, who may be drafted into armed service by his country at any time." My father had to wait for another two years until he obtained Swiss citizenship and was allowed to take his bride home.

This anecdote illustrates the Swiss exceptionalism better than any sociological summary could possibly do. Switzerland is in many ways a country apart, and the Swiss very strongly feel that they have their unique vocation. The conviction of my grandmother that even a major war in the nuclear age would leave the country untouched may be utterly naive, but even today many Swiss believe that the country can stay aloof in a sea of global transformations and can, in such questions as European unity, proudly go it alone.

1

Outsiders also credit Switzerland with a number of special characteristics, in various degrees of sophistication. Novices tend to confound Switzerland, a country in central Europe, with Sweden, which is in Scandinavia. Others have a Disneyland notion of a country excelling mainly for its chocolate, cheese, and cowbells. On a more informed note, the peaceful coexistence of several **cultural** and language groups is hailed, or signs of wealth such as a high **per capita income** are cited. *The Economist,* in its international quality-of-living survey in 1993, ranked Switzerland as the best place to live in the world ("Where to Live," 1993–1994). The second rank was given to Germany, with the United States relegated to the eighth. Sense or nonsense of such ranking exercises, of course, depends on the value judgments made by the choice of indicators. But more important than the overall rank is the way its components are related to each other. "Despite Switzerland's overall victory," the survey found, "it does not win outright any of the four individual categories (economic, social, cultural and political). The secret of Switzerland's success is that, in its well-ordered way, it is quite good in most areas. Other countries excel in one category, but fail dismally in another. For instance, America ranks top on cultural factors, but is only 15th on social ones."

The image of a country that studiously avoids extremes will return in many facets. But this book is less concerned with rank and judgment than with a sociological sense of the uniqueness that sets Switzerland apart from other countries with which at the same time it is more closely integrated than it likes to admit. Like *The Economist*, we will survey what is unique and what is similar or common with others, through chapters that portray the major areas of Swiss society. Numbers will be used, not as a final result, but to illustrate internal differentiations as well as degrees of commonality with the larger world. Most specifically Swiss situations, however, will be derived from a very small number of fundamentals. We shall endeavor to see the workings of these few elementary forces in all the major **institutional** realms addressed.

There are three such essential premises on which the argument is built: the size of the country, its central position in Europe, and its protection from what still is the most important historic event of this century, the Second World War. These basic factors are not isolated from others, nor all-determining, nor reducible to single numbers or facts. But they are the backdrop against which just about every aspect of life in Switzerland has developed, consciously or unconsciously.

BASIC THEMES: SMALLNESS, CENTRALITY, CONTINUITY

Switzerland is a small country. Cut it out from the map, and you will find that its major axis, from east to west, measures just about the distance between New York and Washington, and is considerably shorter than a trip from Los Angeles to San Francisco. Seven million people live in Switzerland—fewer than in Greater Los Angeles alone. Being small has momentous consequences: lack of military and political leadership in the European power concert, a dense economic fabric tying Switzerland into the outside world, and immense pressure to specialize in narrow **market niches,** a sharp contrast between foreign media consumption and attachment to local **culture.** Domestic ramifications abound; for example, in all but the largest professional groups, you are bound to meet, in the course of your career, most of the people who count in your field. The presumption of small community extends to the entire country. Good is what is accessible.

Think of gigantic waves rolling against each other in the center of Europe and then breaking on the slopes of the **Alpine mountains.** The waves are the European empire builders, expanding from the plains of France, Germany, and Austria. The area left dry is central Switzerland. The country is composed essentially of the loose ends of larger peoples that their polities were unable to control. The product of failed incorporation in various empires, the Swiss squat the mountain passes between the major wealth-creating regions of the Italic peninsula in the south and Germany, northern France, Belgium, the Netherlands, and Britain in the north. The central position is both geographical and cultural. Zurich is less than 500 miles from Rome, Berlin, Paris, and London. Three of the four Swiss national languages are spoken also in surrounding countries, by a number of people many times the Swiss population. For a drastic comparison, imagine for a moment that the size of the U.S. population were limited to a 15th of all English speakers in the world. Americans would then number about 30 million only, a clear minority in their cultural area, analogous to the relative position of the Swiss. But the mountainous terrain not only has rebuffed empires, it also has fostered cultural diversity and local political autonomy at home. The Swiss version of **democracy** is one of the notable offshoots.

One is tempted to consider size and location as immutable—who will ever move the Alps in historic time?—and therefore systematic factors, whereas events like the world wars appear as passing in time and accidental to the formation of society. But this would be presociological thinking. The fact that the border with Germany still runs along the river Rhine, and not at the Saint Gotthard Pass in central Switzerland, has to do more with the defeat of Adolf Hitler's armies (by the western allies and the Soviet Union, not by the neutral Swiss) than with geography or age-honored sovereignty over 41,293 square kilometers. The protected space that history afforded the Swiss for the elaboration of their society had been intact since the end of the **French Revolution** in 1815; it came within a "hairwidth" of harm's way between 1933 and 1945. Switzerland's unscathed survival is alternatingly glorified in terms of rightful resistance to dictatorship and reviled for the dirty compromises that were part of its survival tactics. But its rarely noticed latent consequences may prove more durable than the moral rectitude of the era. The country became an island of stability with access to cheap capital. An intact production apparatus was rapidly expanded, with capital and knowledge-intensive sectors, and with extensive use of foreign labor. Thirty years after World War II, a Swiss middle class (see **social classes**) was in place, unparalleled in breadth and wealth but for very few countries. But the same continuity unbroken by war trauma that gave wings to the economy has slowed down the cultural development of the Swiss people, and recently has fueled international debate over the cooperation of Swiss banks and authorities with the **Nazi** war machine.

The reader will discover the basic themes—smallness, **centrality,** continuity—varied in the main chapters that follow. The basic thesis of the book is that Switzerland, thriving in the favor of its geopolitical niche for 150 years, has amassed unique institutional features. Elaborate power-sharing arrangements between its major communities underpinned the peaceful cohabitation of several language and religious communities. Since the sixties, changes in the foreign environment as well as in the inner fabric of Swiss society have been accelerated. The amount of adaptive policies now required is taxing the capacity for consensus and coordination. If a major crisis occurred in central Europe, it could rupture the Swiss political system and even test national cohesion. If we assume a stable evolution around the country, the Swiss are likely to remain in the league of wealthy nations, but are bound to live with much stronger tensions between modernity and tradition than hitherto known.

THE PLAN OF THE BOOK

The book opens with a short chapter that places Switzerland in the European landscape and history and gauges the extent of **urbanization** within the country. A longer chapter on **culture** and **social structure** follows. It will attempt an approximation of the Swiss national character. The Janus face of Swiss culture is shown: Its tendency to look backward is strangely complemented with a very active role in which the state promotes the self-analysis of a free nation. The coexistence of several language communities is investigated. Although inequalities between them are not negligible, they are much smaller than those that operate on a hierarchical dimension. Despite a broad middle class, social inequalities in Switzerland are strong. Those that affect women have proven to be particularly resilient because they are being reinforced by social, economic, as well as cultural factors. All that is happening amid global transformations that force openness to the larger world; this in turn induces cultural and political strain.

Compared to the disquietude that economic and cultural change bring about, several of the basic **institutions** in Swiss society look strangely placid. Churches and other religious groups, schools, universities, and industrial apprenticeships, as well as family life, have kept changing, but at a pace that on several indicators appear more sluggish than in the United States or other advanced nations. Their relative stability means that the Swiss are more worried with their economic future than with any basic values problems.

The Swiss polity receives extensive attention. It has been said that socially Switzerland was not exceptional in any significant degree, was somewhat exceptional for its economy, and was markedly so in the political structures and processes (Borner, Brunetti, and Straubhaar 1990: 68). Space is given to fathoming out the major traditions—**direct democracy, federalism, neutrality**—that are at the root of the special institutions. We will understand not only that Switzerland does not have a strong executive president, but that this office is so unimportant that many Swiss do not even know the name of their president. Americans who complain about the lobbying power of **special-interest groups** will be dismayed to find that the participation of business associations and trade unions in Swiss government has been elevated to a virtuous routine. We will also look at **social movements** that challenge the established agendas.

While the Swiss do politics very much as an inward-looking business, their economy is wide open to the outside world. You cannot buy a Swiss-brand PC; the country does not have the clout to start entirely new industries, but many of us click with a mouse that incorporates Swiss technology. A small country, Switzerland has to devise particular strategies for survival in a competitive world economy, and its economic position is strong but far from secure. Very advanced export-oriented industries contrast with a domestic sector that is surviving thanks to protective measures. This duality has repercussions on other areas of society.

The panorama of Swiss society concludes with a chapter on **social problems** and with a brief outlook to the future. The heading "Social Problems" was chosen in deference to American sociological tradition; the Swiss themselves rarely see a need to group such diverse areas as poverty, immigration, drug addiction, AIDS, and others in a broad generic category and prefer to treat them separately while acknowledging the links that may exist between them in reality.

ACT LOCALLY, AND YOU WILL ALSO THINK LOCALLY

The way information for this book could be found has been influenced by the study object's own behavior. In 1992, the Swiss people rejected a proposition to join the **European Economic Area.** This extremely momentous decision has added to political and economic isolation. Also, since the fall of the Berlin wall in 1989, Switzerland has been competing for international attention with an increasing number of European countries. One of the side effects is a growing islandization of knowledge. International comparisons in widely read journals such as *The Economist* include Switzerland less and less often. This book tries to present comparative data wherever meaningful, but some of the desired data are not available. Many statements are also couched in concepts that are uniquely Swiss and want explanation. For example, I occasionally make comparisons between richer and poorer, urban and rural cantons. **Cantons** are political subdivisions and may not be familiar with all readers.

This and other foreign concepts are explained in a glossary and are highlighted in the text, some of them in several chapters.

Material for further study is unfortunately limited by the language factor. There is not much available in the way of English-language books on Switzerland. A small number of sites have sprung up on the World Wide Web with links to documents in English as well. Often, however, a search may be more efficient using a World Wide Web search machine and specific key words.

CONCLUSION

The Swiss strongly think that their country is unique. History and a good number of institutional arrangements support their claim. But in a less flattering perspective, the uniqueness of Switzerland is simply due to the fact that the surrounding empires, by historic accident, did not absorb the country into their own folds. In that sense, it is no different from other small countries in Europe. What does make Switzerland truly unique, then, is its ability to navigate peacefully through nearly two centuries and translate this into the kind of prosperous society that, despite isolation and stuffiness, the Swiss as well as many outsiders still find an enviable place to live.

FURTHER READINGS

Hilowitz, Janet Eve, ed., *Switzerland in Perspective*. New York: Greenwood Press, 1990. Contains a number of contributions to subjects not widely covered in this volume, such as youth, crime control, trade unions, and Switzerland's image abroad.

Swiss Review of World Affairs, a publication of the Verlag Neue Zürcher Zeitung, P.O. Box CH-8021, Zürich, Switzerland, exposits Swiss views of world and national affairs.

Readers who command German may find, with the same publisher, Verlag Neue Zürcher Zeitung, a volume of essays on recent problems and perspectives: Spillmann, Kurt R. and Rolf Kieser, eds. *Blickpunkt Schweiz*, Zurich: Verlag Neue Zürcher Zeitung, 1995.

CHAPTER 1

History and Geography

This chapter situates Switzerland in time and space. It defines size, neighborhood with other countries, and types of landscapes. A nutshell history leads through key events and eras that proved formative for social structure as well as for the people's own conception of their place in the world. Over time, physical space became filled with human settlements that form a distinctive pattern on the Swiss map. Together, these elements supply basic coordinates for anchoring the description of Swiss society.

AGE AND SIZE: OLD, SMALL, AND ROBUST

An Area the Size of Massachusetts, Connecticut, and Rhode Island

Switzerland is a landlocked country in the central part of the **Alpine mountains.** Its surface is roughly that of Massachusetts, Connecticut, and Rhode Island combined (41,293 sq km, or 15,941 sq mi). It borders on Germany in the north, France in the west, Italy in the south, Austria in the east—all of which are larger than Switzerland—as well as the tiny Principality of Liechtenstein in the east. The country is drained by four major rivers, each associated chiefly with one of four neighboring countries and ending in a different sea: the Rhine with Germany and the North Sea, the Rhône with France and the western Mediterranean, the Ticino with Italy and the Adriatic Sea, and finally the Inn with Austria and the Black Sea. About 60 percent of the area is taken up by the mountains and hills of the **Alps,** which reach an elevation as high as 15,203 feet. To their north, the densely populated **Midlands** stretch between the two major lakes, Geneva in the west and Constance in the northeast. In the northwest, toward France, the **Jura** mountains claim some 10 percent of the national territory.

Travelers through Switzerland will, therefore, form a very different impression depending on the traverse. When you travel on the east–west

FIGURE 1

Switzerland, Its Landscapes, Major Cities, and Surrounding
Countries

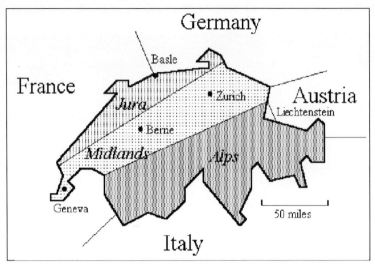

Source: A. Benini, 1997.

axis, you likely set out from one of the major lakes and end your Swiss
journey at the other, thus feeling that you move through an interior space
naturally bounded at both ends, and with Berne, the capital city, roughly
halfway. Not so for the north–south course, where the breathtaking event
is the crossing of a major obstacle, the Alps, in the middle, and the fron-
tiers that mark entry and exit are far less dramatic. Whichever route you
choose, however, will not take more than a few hours to complete.

Switzerland was founded as a tribal **Confederation** in the year
1291. As such, it would claim over 700 years of historic continuity. We
shall see in the chapter on culture that the year 1291 competes with
two other foundational marks in the identity of the Swiss. In 58 BC, the
Helvetians, a Celtic people, were defeated by the Romans, who conquered the region of modern Switzerland. In 1848, a modern federalist
state was founded, absorbing the formerly sovereign tribal states.
They became what we nowadays call the **cantons,** the political tier in
the middle between the **Confederation** and the local **communes.** Table 1
displays the current size and population as well as the age of membership and the major languages in the order in which statistical tables
are usually handled for Swiss cantons.

Undisturbed but for the French Revolution

But in the understanding of many Swiss, the nation goes back to 1291,
and they, therefore, consider themselves citizens of a much older country than the United States. Switzerland went through gradual territorial

TABLE 1

The Cantons of Switzerland

Canton	Area (sq mi)	Year Population, Dec. 1994	Admitted to Confederation	Cantonal Languages
Zurich	667	1,168,567	1351	German
Berne	2,302	941,747	1353	German, French
Lucerne	577	337,941	1332	German
Uri	416	35,933	1291	German
Schwyz	351	120,576	1291	German
Obwalden*	189	30,958	1291	German
Nidwalden*	107	35,983	1291	German
Glarus	265	39,388	1352	German
Zug	92	90,412	1352	German
Fribourg	645	222,227	1481	French, German
Solothurn	305	237,338	1481	German
Basle—Town*	14	197,054	1501	German
Basle—Country*	200	251,259	1501	German
Schaffhausen	115	73,894	1501	German
Appenzell Outer Rhodes*	94	54,227	1513	German
Appenzell Inner Rhodes*	67	14,742	1513	German
Saint Gall	782	440,744	1803	German
Grisons	2,743	184,155	1803	German, Romansh, Italian
Aargovia	542	523,114	1803	German
Thurgovia	383	220,335	1803	German
Ticino	1,086	302,131	1803	Italian
Vaud	1,240	602,099	1803	French
Valais	2,017	269,341	1815	French, German
Neuchatel	310	164,176	1815	French
Geneva	109	391,699	1815	French
Jura	323	68,979	1979	French
Total	**15,940**	**7,019,019**		

*Denotes a half-canton.

Source: *Switzerland* (Berne: Kümmerly and Frey, 1995), p. 23.

expansion, complementing its rural heartland in the mountains with more prosperous city-states in the Midlands. Nominally, the country remained part of the Holy Roman Empire of German Nation, as Germany (and partly Italy) were called in the Middle Ages, and political disputes as well as mercenary traditions brought the Swiss into frequent armed conflict with neighbors. Three centuries of early nation building almost came undone in the **Reformation** when four internal wars between Catholics and Protestants created a deep rift in Swiss society. The European powers formally recognized the Swiss independence in only 1648.

The 18th century saw renewed patriotism overcoming denominational contention, but also the invasion of French Revolutionary armies. In 1798, they created what was to remain the only, and temporary, suspension of national continuity. In 1815, the Swiss **neutrality** was internationally recognized, an asset that helped to weather the European imperialism of the next 150 years. Political and economic modernization went hand in hand in the 19th century. Switzerland became a unified sovereign state in 1848, opening domestic boundaries and creating a framework for railroad expansion to lead the growth process in the second half of the century.

The country is lacking in all natural resources except water power; industrialization therefore followed two opposing trends that would shape society into the 20th century. Many factories were built along streams and rivers, as well as in hilly country, creating elites with part of their power bases in rural areas and with a vested interest in the decentralized political system. At the same time, a large portion of the foreign exchange needed to pay for raw materials was earned by export manufacturers who were leading the technological and, through professional diversification, also the social modernization.

SWISS FRONTIERSMANSHIP: RESPECT FOR VICTIMS OF WAR

In 1859, Henry Dunant, a Swiss businessman from Geneva, was traveling in northern Italy in order to meet the French emperor, who was leading a military campaign against the Austrians. But instead of striking a business deal, Dunant stumbled into a battlefield where 40,000 soldiers were dying, devoid of any medical attention. Dunant, with the help of local women, improvised first aid and comfort for the wounded and dying. Three years later, moved by the horrors of that man-made disaster, he wrote *A Memory of Solferino,* a book that proposed medical aid societies and championed respect for the war-wounded on all sides of armed conflicts (Dunant [1862] 1986). Dunant founded the international Red Cross movement. Also, with diplomatic support from the Swiss Confederation, he obtained international recognition of his humanitarian ideas through what was to become known as the Geneva Conventions for the protection and assistance to war victims.

The expansion of a protected sphere for noncombatants threatened by armed conflict is the closest thing in Swiss history to the

Continued

American concept of a moving frontier. Applied to the same century in which Dunant lived, the original frontier meant an area of free space receding with the advance of human settlement. Taken in that sense, the frontier had been closed already before or around the birth of the Confederation in 1291. It was revived in a social sense when Swiss mercenaries roamed the surrounding empires of the late Middle Ages and again, individually, by emigrants of modern times. When these outlets also closed, some Swiss contributed creatively to moving the frontier to the small scales of space, in technologies such as the scanning tunneling microscope (which, so to say, "sees" individual atoms) and molecular engineering.

But much larger groups have struggled with the humanitarian frontier. This is not a geographical or technological, but a normative space, as befits a conservative country like Switzerland. Against all odds of hatred and destruction, International Humanitarian Law seeks to uphold minimal respect for all civilians, prisoners, and wounded persons in war. Virtually all states of the world have signed the Geneva Conventions and instruct their armed forces personnel in the comportment they demand. The Red Cross has grown into the largest social movement, with an estimated 250 million members worldwide. The International Committee of the Red Cross, based in Geneva, operates assistance programs for the victims of some 50 contemporary armed conflicts. One of the largest Swiss multinationals with over 6,000 employees, the Committee's humanitarian frontiersmanship is just as much about ideals as about physical relief. At present it is a leader in the campaign for the universal ban of antipersonnel mines that maim and kill thousands of innocents every year.

Lasting Peace, and an Extreme Threat

Switzerland has enjoyed continuous peace and economic growth since 1848. It has no comparable experience to the American Civil War or to the communist revolution. It also has no modern colonial experience. Armed neutrality was maintained in both world wars. Class struggle between workers and capitalists was intense in the first decades of this century. In larger urban-industrial centers, a pronounced **socialist** milieu developed, complete with social-democratic city governments, newspapers, cultural centers, and cooperative housing estates. Under the threat from fascist Germany and Italy, employers and trade unions moved closer to each other. From 1940 to 1944, the country was surrounded by fascist armies on all four sides, and an invasion and subsequent incorporation of large parts of Switzerland into an all-Germanic Reich seemed to be only a question of time. In response, immense pressure for Swiss national unity and social conformity developed. It continued to provide a conservative ideological cast up until the late sixties when the major cultural changes in advanced Western countries also would pull along Switzerland. In contrast to the United States, however, where McCarthyism aimed to reverse the New Deal, the Swiss conservatism was less rabid and did not stand in the way of the expanding welfare state and public enterprises. The political **left** was included in government and has remained part of a broad coalition.

Meanwhile, political and economic environments have changed radically again. Swiss enterprises increasingly compete in global markets. European unification has progressed, and with the end of the Cold War, the continent forms an even larger sphere. In 1986, the Swiss people rejected plans to join the **United Nations,** and in 1992 they said no to the **European Economic Area,** which would have given Switzerland and the countries of the **European Union** mutual access to their markets. Access to the archives of the former Soviet Union has given fresh impetus to investigate the cooperation between Germany and the neutral countries during the Second World War, and since 1996 international outcry over the handling of Holocaust victim assets by Swiss banks has increasingly disconcerted the Swiss in their "business as usual" attitudes. Once again, Switzerland looks like a mountain not yet covered by the waves of the sea. But its society is not impervious to the tides, and we shall see them at work in every subsequent chapter.

URBANIZATION: A EUROPEAN METROPOLIS WITH GREEN SPOTS

Cities That Grow into Neighboring Countries

Switzerland's 6,873,673 residents in 1990 lived in almost every conceivable kind of crowd and solitude, from the packed high-rise apartment towers in suburban Zurich to the herdsman cottage on a secluded mountain pasture. But the true measure of daily living was supplied by the mixed urban **agglomerations,** the isolated towns and villages and scattered homesteads that one traverses on the major highway and railroad axes. In just five hours, the intercity train covers the east–west journey between Lake Constance and Lake Geneva, which bound the country in their symbolic symmetry. No major city of the kind we associate with New York, Paris, or Tokyo is found, and at every point the traveler can make out a human settlement no farther than half a mile afield. This is the Midlands, the nation's economic, social, and (largely also) political heartland. It is as densely populated as some of the most compacted European countries (around 370 persons per square kilometer; the Netherlands has 355) and more than 15 times the density of some of the mountain regions or the sparsely populated larger European states like Sweden. From the outside, therefore, Switzerland may look like one major urban space, a metropolis in central Europe. And in fact, that is a widely shared perception, by virtue of the rich international connections that the Swiss financial and industrial businesses have built. Some of the urban agglomerations extend into neighboring countries: Geneva into France, Basle at the "Three-Nation Corner" into France and Germany, Lugano into Italy. Internally, however, we see a finely grained pattern composed of large, medium, and small agglomerations. Size again is a relative matter. The Geneva agglomeration, for example, one of the largest, is formed of 71 politically autonomous communes, with 424,028 inhabitants. Within the agglomerations, green spaces are preserved, regional planning policies direct growth to lesser centers, and public transport keeps jobs and schools more easily available. It seems only a question of time until the entire Midlands will have grown into one agglomeration stretching from lake to lake.

Strong Population Growth, Due to Immigrants

And urban growth there has been. In 1990, 69 percent of the population lived in what the Federal Statistical Office classified as urban environments, up from 62 percent in 1980. Of the 48 urban agglomerations, almost a third have emerged since 1980. Isolated urban communes, surrounded by rural areas, are nowadays the exception. Most of this growth in urban habitat was necessary to accommodate rapid population growth. Between 1980 and 1990, the resident population grew by 8.0 percent,

Open Switzerland: Italians and Swiss meet at an "Alp Feast" (mountain party) in the Canton of Ticino; photographer, Matthias Wehrlin.

much faster than in the previous decade (1.5 percent) and faster than in surrounding Europe (e.g., France, 5.2 percent; Italy, 2.2 percent).

Thus, Switzerland is largely an urban society, albeit one that does without mega-cities. But again things are not that simple. Not all the growth took place in the urban centers, though. Some of it followed the "dynamic snowbelt" of the Alpine mountains and their neighboring districts. Demography, it seems, was shaped by two forces. Switzerland lies on the main economic axis from London to northern Italy, which injects vitality primarily to the so-called Golden Triangle. This is the area that the central Midlands form with Basle and is part of the north–south axis. Intersecting with that is the decentralized development of tourism and new industry in the French, Swiss, German and Austrian mountain regions (Schuler and Joye 1995: 120); in other words, an east–west commonality. Beneath the larger regions, the maps reveal a finer grain. Communes that have lost population are very often next door to towns that grew by more than 40 percent in one decade. In many cases, suburbanization was at work, creating dormitory communities while the jobs remained in the cities. In some rural areas, the tourist industry or specialized manufacturers created new jobs that attracted more people to live there.

The question then is whether the demographic ups and downs expressed the mobility of the large middle class, rich enough to follow new opportunities and make residential choices. To an extent, that seems true. Until about 1950, internal migrations followed a classical pattern. Rural and Catholic cantons had high birth rates; their surplus population would migrate to the urban-industrial centers where fertility had already decreased. After 1980, that pattern was reversed. Those cantons that were attracting more residents also had higher birth rates. These areas offered more and better residential and/or job opportunities of which young families could take advantage. Commuter statistics confirm that picture. In 1960, only one in five Swiss worked outside his or her commune of residence. This figure has since jumped by 10 percentage points in every decade, with one in two workers nowadays commuting. Society has indeed become more mobile.

In yet another important aspect, the 8 percent population increase was not the outcome of individual autonomy. A full two-thirds of the growth was due to fresh **immigration** and to children born to resident foreigners, a census finding that shocked the Swiss. The growth in foreign population reminded them that asylum seekers from countries in civil war (former Yugoslavia is nearby), economic migrants from the Third World, and cultural differences in lifestyles did not stop at the national borders. Foreigners often have more limited choice of jobs and residences, and in some of the larger cities, residential segregation and mild urban decay are nowadays conspicuous. The less well-to-do among the Swiss, particularly among the elderly, also get stuck in situations of decreasing opportunity. It has, therefore, been predicted that the large urban spaces will create major social disparities internally. These would be no less stark than the traditional urban–rural differences that Switzerland knew before the Second World War (Schuler and Joye 1995: 169–70). But that is a future scenario; in the early nineties, Switzerland simply has not known the kind of urban blight that condemns many US inner cities.

PERIPHERAL IMPRESSIONS: THE VILLAGE CATTLE SHOW

A stiff, cold wind blows down from the nearby hills as we walk between rows of cows and heifers presented at the 1996 annual cattle show. Most of the farmers in Schönengrund, a village of 350 souls, are there to watch the experts of the cantonal department of agriculture score their best animals, and a number of them are sporting their traditional herdsman's best in bright red and yellow. The owner of the commune's only remaining breeding bull has gathered a small crowd around him, arguing that artificial insemination is no longer favored in the eyes of the health-conscious. Across the road, some ambulant dealers have set up their wares, but nobody seems to be buying.

It is not only because of the unfriendly weather that the mood is unusually sullen. By midday, most farmers have fled to the warmth of the Krone Inn, where beer and wine make them more talkative. Some are treating their young sons and friends from outside to barley soup and platters of meat. The only woman in evidence (other than the two waitresses) is not eating; the department secretary, she busies herself copying the experts' scores onto huge ledgers. A dog circles between tables as if chasing after an invisible ghost. For those present, of course, the ghost is none else but mad-cow disease, which has driven the beef market into collapse. These farmers survive on an average of 22 cows per farm; their incomes have dwindled by 30 percent since 1990, despite dairy prices that are 70 percent higher than in the European Economic Area. Many have overinvested in machinery and are compelled to find part-time jobs in other sectors. But the village offers few opportunities: a machine shop with 30 workers and a family business in construction are the only nonfarm industries at this **peripheral** location.

The men in the Krone resent being penalized for a mysterious disease that frightens producers and consumers alike, but leaves a stigma on them. "After all, it's the big industries that have polluted the North Sea," one of them observes, but his logic is lost on his colleagues. Suddenly, without warning, several red and yellow

Sources: Visit to Schönengrund, Appenzell-Outer Rhodes, September 24, 1996. Hans Knaus, personal communications, St. Gallen, November 1996.

Continued

men start a *yodel*, a deep, resounding song handed down many generations. They sing beautifully, with closed eyes and in reverence to the old spirit of community and friendship, for a moment driving out cold, disease, and abandonment.

The scene is imbued with irony. While the small farmers yodeling away their anxiety struggle to survive in the rural economy, most outsiders visiting the Krone Inn instantly feel at home with the core symbolism of the nation. Switzerland, for all its modern transformations, is holding on to a self-image that has remained rural. Proud of their technological position, many Swiss, nevertheless, deep down feel anchored to villages, forests, and mountains. They find it hard to admit that Switzerland is largely an urban society. Schönengrund may be at the periphery of the modern economy, but it fits right in the center of the Swiss culture.

CONCLUSION

Despite being modern, with all the technological and social change that transformed Switzerland, this is a country governed by a sense of constancy. It counts itself as an old nation, one that has managed to stay clear of the major historic disasters that have befallen its unfortunate neighbors, notably the two world wars. In areas of gradual change, however, Swiss society has widely participated. This concerns, in this chapter, urbanization and population movements. The result is paradoxical: A country with more than half of its area covered by mountains and hills also holds one of the larger European metropolitan areas. This is the core region of Switzerland, the Midlands, stretching from east to west as an almost continuous tapestry of cities, towns, and villages. You might expand that statement to say that one of the core regions in the center of Europe is formed by this relatively small area within this small country, of an economic and social significance that is totally out of proportion with its geographical size.

FURTHER READING

Im Hof, Ulrich. *Geschichte der Schweiz und der Schweizer.* Basel and Frankfurt a.M.: Helbing & Lichtenhahn, 1986. A classic of modern Swiss historiography.

Culture and Social Structure

On a sunny springtime morning in 1966, I sat beside the driver of an old truck, overwhelmed with awe and joy as it grumbled and teetered up the steep road and across the railroad tracks to the cooperative housing estate into which we were moving from the very humble no-bathroom apartment of my childhood. Years later, father would tease that he could figure out his lifetime upward mobility to be exactly 200 feet in altitude. But it was all too clear that not only had we moved physically from the "lower village" to the good side of the railroad tracks, but also that the one-mile trip in the house moving truck expressed one of the major social advancements in the life of my family. Outwardly, not much changed. Father would continue to walk to the textile factory, mother did part-time work in a municipal bath, and I got around by bike and public transport. But the quality of life dramatically improved for us. Within a year, we acquired a refrigerator, TV, and telephone, and I had my own study to help me prepare for the university, something that had not been in the reach of my working-class parents.

While I personally tie our progress to memories of the truck trip, hundreds of thousands of Swiss may remember with different images their prosperity during the Golden Thirty Years 1945–1975. But many will rave about some kind of conveyance that carried them on an upward journey. The Swiss sociologists Levy, Joye, Guye, and Kaufmann in a forthcoming study of social **stratification** in Switzerland use the elevator metaphor. The Golden era experienced such strong economic growth, they say, that virtually the whole Swiss nation was packed into the elevator. Not all people would get out on the same floor; most would travel up a similar distance, keeping the initial rank order and leaving the spaces on the lower end to be filled with new people who entered through the main door, such as immigrants and, in the working world, women.

A child of that era, I was lucky to have upward rides on both the physical truck and Levy's figurative elevator. Both happened because there were many changes in social positions. And what is equally important, they were made possible not only by economic growth, but also by Swiss culture. Examples of this *abounded around the housing cooperative of my youth. It had largely been financed by an industrial enterprise that felt, in their Swiss ways, that responsibility for their workers did not stop at the paycheck. The president of the cooperative happened to be my primary school teacher, who also took an interest in the well-being of his students beyond academic concerns. The railway line was, and still is, part of a massive government-operated public transport system, a way of saying that society needs to help all people get around. Both created positions—for renters and for commuting employees, that is—and both were value statements.*

*Thus, as in every other society, **social structure** and **culture** in Switzerland are closely intertwined and mutually supportive. This chapter deals with both as equally important aspects of society. It shows how Swiss culture is the sediment of history but is molded also by contemporary social structure. Social structure, on the other hand, operates on cultural premises, such as the particular national education systems. Considerable space is given to a well-known part of Swiss culture, the coexistence of several language communities. Also the question is explored whether there is a special Swiss national character. On the side of social structure, the extent of inequality and forms of mobility are at the center of inquiry. The importance of foreigners for the position of the Swiss and different access to institutional areas for men and women are brought to light. Since 1970, change in both social structure and culture has become faster, and we study the effects of the acceleration in both areas.*

CULTURE: FACTORS OF CONSTANCY

"There Is No Switzerland"

Continuity, I said in the Introduction, is one of the defining themes of Switzerland. As I move toward exploring factors of constancy in the cultural area, let me nevertheless caution the reader with an anecdote that seems to emphasize the opposite of cultural stability. In 1991 Switzerland was to celebrate the 700th anniversary of the **Confederation.** For years before, plans and financial provisions were made for a number of big events. In an atmosphere of enthusiasm and openness, Swiss artists were asked to play a leading role. Then a political scandal broke. A startled public learned that the secret service had spied, for years, on thousands of citizens. It also had classified as potential subversives artists who were now being invited to lend their talents to national festivities. Several artists withdrew; others boycotted all public cultural activities. Those who contributed artwork to the Sevilla World Exhibition a year later presented their country under the negative heading: "There is no Switzerland." Many Swiss took it as an extremely unflattering provocation. Cutting government budgets for the arts, revenge was taken against those who bit the hand that fed them (Frauchiger 1995: 48–49).

This episode, better than any theory, highlights how volatile Swiss national identity can be, to the point that self-adoration as one of the oldest democracies gives way to denial of her own true existence. This, as I said, should serve as a note of caution in any attempt to define values and symbols as typically Swiss. Values lead opportunistic lives; they change together with social structure and, more quickly even, with interests and situations. But if values are volatile, parts of the social environment that favor some values over others are, nevertheless, remarkably stable. This is true notably of geography and history.

A Reminder: Switzerland as a Special Case in History

For a point of departure, let us repeat the well-known: Switzerland lives in the heart of Europe. It holds a crossroad position, important particularly on the north–south axis that links the rich northern European belt with the Italian peninsula. In the center rise the Alpine mountains, no longer untrammeled nature but still the immovable backdrop to everything human that grows and dies in the valleys and in the cities of the plains. The rivers that drain them eventually flow into four different seas; miraculously, each of the watersheds is inhabited chiefly by a populace of different language. Three of these communities straddle borders with larger countries; the size of the Swiss segments and the fact that they were not annexed by their mightier language consorts is the outcome of a long drawn-out, sometimes turbulent historical equation. What the European powers eventually recognized is a country divided by physical and cultural features and united solely by its will to be Swiss.

It is this ambivalence between geographical *centrality* and *peripheral* status in the face of empires that defines Switzerland. Internally, the pattern is replicated, again under no small influence of the landscape: the rugged mountain areas are not the ones that harbor the centers of trade and power, and these have been obliged to grant far-reaching autonomy to small local communities. In addition to space, the temporal pattern has been determining. The country is old, or, more correctly, there were early key events that allowed it to be defined as old. As described earlier, the Swiss Confederation, founded in 1291, saw its continuous existence interrupted not until 500 years later, only once, and then only briefly during the French Revolution. Its reorganization as a modern nation-state in the mid-19th century preceded the culmination of culturally based nationalisms in Europe, and thereby permitted the construction of a collective identity around the depth of common history that accommodated different religious and language communities. Most momentously, however, Switzerland was spared the horrors of two world wars. Under no obligation to cope with massive guilt, loss, and damage, it flew ahead of other nations on the wings of peace and, sometimes, self-righteousness.

Just as culture is made up of the sedimented part of history, so contemporary social structure molds it. Hardly a note is sung without at first somebody being appointed conductor of the choir, and chances to become conductor incite the musical to try harder. In Switzerland, the consolidation of the large majority of citizens in a broad middle class and the absence of huge urban agglomerations may be singled out. The close **social integration** of the natives makes for conformity in cultural expression. Also, in a rich country, it offers a lot of money and time for special events and voluntary associations. On the other hand, a small population may prevent critical mass from building for excellence. In earlier times, Switzerland had no princely courts and few rich arts patrons. The lack of feudal traditions also reinforces the middle class and population effects in the cultural realms.

CONSEQUENCES: SWISS NATIONAL CHARACTER

Few Philosophers, Many Teachers

A nation's personality cannot simply be inferred from its environment. Yet many of the Swiss cultural characteristics seem likely or plausible in the light of the more important premises. Thus, when we remember the small size of the country, its dependency on the economic and political currents of powerful neighbors, and its developed power-sharing mechanisms at home, then it is hardly surprising to find a marked **pragmatism** pervading most realms of Swiss life. The Swiss have not been noted as creators of grand philosophical and scientific systems. An exception is found in the city of Geneva, which, through Jean Calvin (1509–1564), one of the most influential theologians of the Reformation, established itself as a city of international radiance, later to play host to the French enlightenment, the Red Cross movement, and the United Nations. But many Swiss did contribute prolifically to existing disciplines and professions. The list of Swiss Nobel Prize winners is impressive.

A parallel may be drawn with the "first user" strategy in Swiss technology development. The country is too small to lead new strategic systems; it buys them when they come to the market and mixes them with native skills. In the process, the Swiss have accumulated pedagogical talent, the gift to organize for the transmission of skills rapidly. Its most mundane expression is the apprenticeship, which combines practical training in factories and offices with vocational college instruction— for well-defined trades, not for exploration of new fields. But if their own **venture capital,** both financial and philosophical, has remained modest, the Swiss have time and again been happy to serve as meeting places for ideas. Einstein taught here. During the years of fascism, the Schauspielhaus in Zurich was the "last bastion of free German language theater" (Coordinating Commission for the Presence of Switzerland Abroad [CCPSA] 1993a: 3). In recent years, Davos, a mountain resort, has hosted jamborees of the world's political, economic, and cultural elites. Geneva is more of an international meeting place than a traditional Swiss city. The crossroad function has survived into the age of information technology.

Numerous Local Views,
Universal Distaste for Extremes

The impotency that a small country often suffered around the great and mighty and the witnessing of major destruction in the wars that engulfed their neighbors made the Swiss deeply anticonflict. They take pride in the peaceful living together of diverse communities. They like to think of themselves as a bunch of **multilinguals** to a point that is rarely validated by actual language proficiency. The protection of minorities has its considerable costs (e.g., by the multiplication of education systems), which in the spirit of tolerance are gladly underwritten. The political elite go about their business discretely and are largely exempt from the kind of close scrutiny to which leaders in American public life are subjected. The writer Adolf Muschg once said that the Swiss have a "deep-seated fear of all that which is explicit and well articulated" (Kriesi 1995: 8), in contrast to the American abhorrence for the concealed. Those who point out the existence of conflict or oppose consensus decisions deemed final risk being ostracized. The reviled Swiss banking secret is defended not only by the rich gnomes in the vaults of money-laundering institutes but just as adamantly by the blue collar worker who, 10 years ago, withheld a trifle sum from his taxable income returns.

The large autonomy that towns and villages have enjoyed for centuries has conditioned the Swiss to **communitarian** models of life. For many, the living reality first of all is the local **commune.** This varies slightly between the language communities, as we shall see later, but localist orientations, valuing personal acquaintance and face-to-face contact, have remained strong even within some neighborhoods of urban agglomerations. When I grew up, the strict norm was to greet each and every person crossing paths in the streets, stranger or acquaintance, with a clear and loud, *"Gruetzi."* This is less universally followed nowadays, but has by far not disappeared. Modern **federalism** has continued the localist flair of Swiss culture, and also the players in the protected domestic sector of the economy empathize easily with their local partners and protectors. Even just to enter the fray, one has to be found worthy by one's close neighbors: One gains Swiss citizenship by the grace of a commune or **canton** that agrees to naturalize him or her, not by meeting the criteria of a distant federal bureaucracy.

Cultural conformities in the lingering image of a closely knit local society have been helped by the strength of the middle class. In their self-appraisal, large portions of the population lean toward the center. This is true of politics (Melich 1991: 41), despite the historically strong **left–right** dimension in voter behavior, as well as of other aspects of life. In contrast to the United States, the Swiss upper class refrains from ostentatious display of wealth; the media pay little attention to the private lives of the rich and glitzy. Egalitarian and **socialist** traditions have creatively interacted with the ethos of liberty and self-responsibility. A well-functioning social security and welfare system keeps at least the Swiss citizens from falling into bottomless holes (while policies toward foreigners are harsher). The cultural presumption is that society has a responsibility for every Swiss to enjoy a decent life. No politician can hope to gain votes by blaming particularly vulnerable citizens, such as unwed mothers. A readiness to censure those who seem to be standing outside the middle ground, self-consciousness in attire, gait, and sentiment, and the coldness that foreign visitors notice in Swiss public demeanor has traditionally been the other side of the coin. Your neighbors closely observe the way you hang your laundry or wash your car and the frequency with which you receive guests, and will not hesitate to share "strange things" with others. Not surprisingly, a well-integrated society has a large segment of members who consider themselves happy persons. In 1989, only 7 percent of a national poll said they were not very happy or not happy at all (Melich 1991: 16–18). The percentage was higher among those who lacked elements of the middle-class status. As many as 12 percent among those who had only primary school education said they were not happy with their lives. With so many of the lowly jobs being held by foreigners, lower-class Swiss citizens may find it harder to gain the respect of their relevant others.

THE FORCE OF MYTHS

How Old Are You, Mother Helvetia?

Melich calls Switzerland "saturated with ancient values" (1991: 8). Indeed, the age and force of the myths around which national identity has remained firm to this day are astounding. As the Swiss could not rely on one common culture, language, or ethnicity for nation-building (Linder 1994: 17), they substituted national symbols, history, and myths, and in the 19th century also the federal polity, as common anchor points. The ultimate exploit was to construct a common ancestry that shared only one trait with the diverse cultural groups making up Switzerland: the same territory.

The **Helvetians,** a Celtic, pre-Christian people, fulfilled that function. They left the area of what is now Switzerland in 58 BC and were decisively vanquished by the Romans. By the time Switzerland was founded in 1291, the Helvetians had been extinct as a nation for more than a thousand years. They left few memories—Poseidonius (100 BC) called them "rich in gold, but peaceful" (Kreis 1993: 57)—and no written heritage. That made them conveniently indifferent to language, **Germanic** and **Romanic** tribal, and Christian denominational interests. The Helvetians endowed Switzerland with the feminine side of national identity, in the form of the mythical **"Mother Helvetia,"** and with its official name in diplomatic relations, "Confoederatio Helvetica" in Latin. But above all, the **myth** did some artificial aging to the country, establishing historical precedence over other, presumably younger, neighbors.

A Celebrated Terrorist

The masculine side of the foundation myth is supplied by the figures of William Tell, who murdered the tyrannical bailiff who had forced him to shoot an apple off his son's head, and of the three Fathers of the **Confederation,** who swore, on August 1, 1291, to create a free nation. Interestingly, the myth of William Tell as liberator was cast into its modern form only in the 18th century and then by a foreigner, the German national poet Friedrich Schiller. In the same era, the dialogue between Swiss and foreign literary figures helped to implant yet another element of national identity: the grandeur and beauty of the mountain scenery. That the mountains were not so much the source of poverty and hardship for those condemned to live on their slopes, but rather of simplicity, bucolic joys, and reverence of the Creator, was a new social definition. It would depend on upper-class tourists of the European romantic movement for its final acceptance at home.

The two national myths coexist, but are not always in equal favor. The Tell myth, actively violent and victorious, lost some of its integration capacity when the denominational struggle weakened the value of the foundation history of the Catholic central cantons. The Helvetian myth, on the other hand, is fraught with defeat, the singular case of a nation tracing its origins back to a people that has long disappeared and, what it more, was outright annihilated in its identity when it transgressed borders. It told the Swiss to stay at home and to avoid the kind of ethnic intolerance to which other European nations fell prey in the 19th and first half of the 20th centuries.

The simultaneous loser and winner myths express a polarity that has often been remarked about the Swiss identity: its perennial vacillation between conceit and fear, between boastfulness and self-doubt, between forceful gesture and denial of their own existence (Frauchiger 1995: 28). But both concur in another respect: They go well with a culture that is primarily backward-looking.

A STATE ACTIVE IN CULTURAL AFFAIRS

The Official Boilerplate of Swiss Virtues

I opened the section on culture with an anecdote on a Switzerland "that does not exist." Surprisingly enough, denial is the position taken not only by discontented artists, but also by part of the Swiss elite, as expressed in a pamphlet of "Pro Helvetia" (a state foundation for the dissemination of Swiss culture): "Ethnographically speaking, there is no Swiss people and no homogeneous Swiss nation. Nor can one talk about a Swiss culture, because various cultures came into contact with one another and even today still overlap. Switzerland has remained a mosaic of world and regional history, religions, languages and dialects, all confined in a very small space." (CCPSA 1993a: 1). But at other times the government has

SWISS IDENTITY LEAPS: MODERN ELECTRICITY AND THE ANCIENT CELTS

In the main body of the text, we show that Swiss national identity is tied to the **Helvetians,** a people of the Celtic culture that dominated much of Europe in the pre-Roman and pre-Germanic era. The Helvetians all but dissolved in the pea soup of nations subjugated and assimilated by the Roman empire. The reference to a people conspicuous by its total absence occasionally has weird local manifestations, one of which has caught up with this author.

Lake Gübsen is an artificial hydroelectric reservoir on the border of the cantons of St. Gallen and Appenzell. It buries trout ponds that the monks of the abbey of St. Gallen, a center of Christian erudition and cultural exchange between the Germanic and Latin worlds, husbanded in the Middle Ages. The destruction of the trout ponds by rebellious Appenzell tribesmen triggered one of the numerous wars between old Switzerland and the Hapsburg princes of Austria and protectors of the abbey. From war, St. Gallen and Appenzell moved on to intense economic cooperation; their cantonal governments own the lake and the power station hidden 250 feet below in the rock of the Sitter gorge.

The place still resounds with old history, public and private. On one of the banks, a 440-year-old farmhouse has been beautifully renovated. The wife of its former tenant arranged for my parents to meet, my mother being Appenzell, my father raised in the city of St. Gallen. My personal attachment to the lake may explain the utter puzzlement that I felt when I found a section of the hiking trail around the lake—lovingly manicured by the utility corporation—fenced with new posters. What from a distance appeared to be an ugly foreign body was a quite artfully painted series of trees. The anonymous authors titled it the "Celtic Tree Horoscope."

Where were the Celts? I looked right—toward St. Gallen, a city with 1300 years of unbroken Christian and Germanic history. I watched left—only to discern on the horizon the "soul-launching pad," a church so nicknamed for its postmodern roof. I lifted my eyes to the Appenzell hills—and saw farmsteads that were not Celtic. Finally, the lake warden helped. He knew that the posters had been created by a group of embroidery designers who lost their jobs in the restructuring of this old St. Gallen industry.

Curiosity made me call their leader. A lady, director of a private foundation for helping the unemployed, explained how she had personally chosen the subject of the exhibition, on account of her long research into the Celtic culture, feminist spirituality, and the lost

Source: Personal interview with the Gübsen Lake warden, and telephone interview with the director, Business House, St. Gallen, August 27–28, 1996.

Continued

mountain peoples. The tree horoscope gave the artists "work and encouragement." My timid observation that St. Gallen was known for different achievements was countered with the assertion that the Germanic culture had lasted "only for a brief moment," and that for outsiders it was difficult to appreciate the merits of Celtic culture. Anyway, they were substantial, as evidenced by the Blessings for the Bees and the Tree of Judgment; for the rest, had not Emperor Charlemagne ordered the mass murder of the Celts?

It would not have been politically correct to argue with a helper of the unemployed. By my questions, the lady seemed to rate me among the sympathizers of ancient ethnic cleansing. But I found it ironic that the defeated of today should be consoled with symbols of a people defeated more than a thousand years ago. The utility corporation practiced cultural tolerance—but who would create new jobs? Also, the return to the Celts and the omission of later cultural universes seemed arbitrary and subjective. So, during my next visit, I turned to the warden again for his opinion on the tree horoscope. "It can't harm," he said. "My family doctor has hung one of them in the waiting room."

served up its own boilerplate of positive Swiss virtues. In 1991, the then-president of the **Confederation,** Flavio Cotti, in a preface of the book *Les valeurs des Suisses The Values of the Swiss,* gave official blessings to a list of core values. It contained democracy, federalism, linguistic pluralism, freedom, the work and education ethos, a government of humane dimensions, and international humanitarianism (Melich 1991: ii).

The Swiss state has also been active in creating and defending what it thought to be good Swiss culture and, in more recent times, in promoting the expression of diversity. For a considerable time after the modern Switzerland was created in 1848, the school and the army were the most important in building and strengthening a national consciousness. Although the army was formed in a strictly federal framework only in 1875 (Kreis 1993: 39), it was approvingly called the "school of the nation." Service was, and to this day is, universal for men. It imbued young men with the discipline and personal hygiene that life in an industrializing, urbanizing Switzerland required. Swiss men took to socks and underwear not out of consideration for their social ambiance but because the army demanded it. Often it was during army service that people came into contact with members of the other language groups. The army also was used to verify compliance of the cantons and communes with their public education mandates. Recruits have undergone, since 1875, scholastic aptitude tests whose results were taken to measure the intellectual progress of the nation. Similarly, health checks on recruits and on soldiers during their periodic training courses were an early form of medical surveillance.

Critics have charged that the cultural contribution of the army amounted to little more than obedient acceptance on the part of the young recruits of working-class misery while the elite benefited from an additional social network through the officers' corps drawn from their ranks. The authoritarianism that seeped from the army into the wider society had its civilian double in the "spiritual defense of the country." This was a propaganda war concept that sought to unite the Swiss population against demoralizing messages from **Nazi** Germany, but later was used to blacken nonconformist thinkers of all hues and cries. Only in the late sixties, when fast economic growth had eroded old values, was the army cut down to stricter political neutrality. A symbolic barrier fell in 1972 when the last cavalry units were abolished. That they had no military value in modern times had long been recognized, but important elite circles had defended the romanticism of horsemanship and of pack animal supply chains amid snow and rock. Since then the army has stopped being one of the chief representatives of the ideals of Switzerland and has settled for a more technical, instrumental role. Rank in the army is no longer a central determinant of social prestige. Whereas the integrative force of the army has lately been reemphasized in the United States, particularly as a professional avenue for lower-class youth, in Switzerland the army has apparently not yet recouped from its loss of cultural functions in recent times.

Big Government Occasionally Creates Good Culture

The cultural activism of the state was no less important on the civilian side. In the 20th century, the singlemost important **institution** has certainly been the several radio and television programs that government-owned corporations operate in each of the three major national languages (with minimum coverage assured also for the tiny **Romansh**-speaking minority). We will look at their market shares more closely in the section on the language communities. Earlier, federal endeavors had addressed other cultural arenas. Soon after 1848 higher technical education was made a priority. That headstart, combined with Swiss pragmatism and economic interests, has maintained the Federal Technical Universities as institutions of excellence. Law and ordinances on the arts and humanities came out later under the threat of European cultural nationalism. But the Confederation has never received a constitutional mandate for "general participation in cultural matters, except for promoting the film industry, nature conservation and protecting the national heritage" (*Switzerland* 1995: 82), despite attempts to create such amendments and despite a wide consensus that the government should sponsor cultural activities of a broad variety. Ad-hoc initiatives have

Closed Switzerland: Nationalist soccer fans close ranks at a local game in Berne.
Photographer, Matthias Wehrlin.

tried to narrow that gap. In 1938, under the direct threat of the Hitler and Mussolini regimes, Romansh was elevated to the status of the fourth national language, and the Swiss dialects within the German language also were ennobled, in order to demarcate Swiss identity more clearly. In 1965, a federal law regulated the operation of the Pro Helvetia Foundation, and 10 years later the Federal Office of Culture was created.

They have since shown that cultural policy can work. Federal monies for the promotion of Swiss movies helped to create an artistic movement that not only brought the language communities in Switzerland into closer dialogue, but also gained the Swiss industry some international recognition. The federal film policy abandoned old patriotic deadweight from the onset, accepting the universalistic values of the new producer generation. These managed to marry humanism and enlightenment to a critical, yet loving picture of their country. The subsidy mechanism obliged producers from all corners of the country to associate and debate their artistic approaches. And the public loved the images even when the new movies from other language regions had to be subtitled. Through the length and width of Switzerland, packed theaters would cheer when the freshly retired farm worker in Yves Yersin's *Minor Fugues* flew on his motorcycle, bought with the first government pension payment, across the skies of his imagination, and would hold their breath when the farmer's daughter made love with the new Italian farmhand in positions that were not from the traditional Swiss book of rules. Contrary to popular novels that more often than not reproduced outdated social stereotypes, the government-supported movies have been both critical and integrative.

Winner Doesn't Take All

While the Confederation takes a look at the whole of the country's cultural situation, cantons and communes subsidize a host of cultural institutions and voluntary associations that follow no unified program but have enough local supporters to appropriate budgets. When you watch a brass band march by, a good bet is to assume that the cost of the uniforms or of some of the instruments was footed by the commune. What council man or woman could afford to vote against it? The decentralized character of the sponsorship activities is manifest also in the budget figures. "In 1988 public expenditure on culture amounted to 1.2 billion francs [roughly one billion US dollars, or $150 per capita]; of this approximately 14 percent came from the Confederation, 35 percent from the cantons and 51 percent from the communes" (CCPSA 1993a: 4). But the same source also notes the preponderance of big cities. The town of Zurich spends almost as much on the promotion of cultural life within its narrow confines as the Confederation does for the entire country. Private and corporate sponsorship of the arts is not negligible either, but comes nowhere near the importance in the United States. It carries no particular tax advantages.

State activity in cultural affairs is promoted also through institutions we would not immediately conceive of as "cultural." Switzerland's strong public enterprises are a case in point—postal services as well as the energy and railway industries. Their cultural functions are more of the latent kind, not written in their charters but still significant for the growth of widely shared meanings. In particular, the Swiss railways are an outstanding cultural icon. The architecture of main stations, the engineering feats in building the **transalpine tunnels,** and the beauty of intercity trains hushing past farmhouses, orchards, and meadows are standard parts of Swiss folklore. The citizens take pride in the railways as a collective achievement and as an egalitarian institution that serves peripheral regions, lower-income groups, commuters, and visitors of other language regions beyond the strict logic of the marketplace. With most government services, people think they get fair value in return for their taxes. Few view the state as oppressive or grossly inefficient. In general the legitimacy of the state is higher in the eyes of Swiss citizens than it is in the United States.

The result has been a very active and varied cultural life in Switzerland since the end of the Second World War. With **fiscal** stringencies in recent years also affecting support in that area, a regressive era may have begun. Public sponsoring has tended to continue the traditional and to become antivisionary. The proportional representation of interest groups on grants allocation committees carries with it the idea that art can be decided by majority rule. Moreover, these bodies lose control when Swiss cultural developments endure the forces of internationalization similar to the economic process. For example, sponsorship of the art of the Alp mountains nowadays calls for European approaches, and for the major revision that German spelling is currently undergoing, it is the Germans who call the tune, also in Switzerland. That the national boundaries of a small country are transparent is even more true of the electronic media.

Most of the cultural arenas (the technical universities and major drama and opera stages are exceptions) have in common that they favor the involvement of the many over the excellence of the few. "To participate is more important than to win" is a common adage. Swiss culture opposes "winner takes all" attitudes. Earlier designed to reinforce the cohesion of a nation constituted by common political will, cultural policy has come to facilitate diversity of expression within the bounds of middle-class propriety. This is in opposition to growing social inequalities that current economic changes are forcing. The Swiss nowadays value the autonomy and competency of individuals to deal with change better than they did some decades ago, but a large majority do not approve of unbridled **capitalism.** The cultural contradictions therefore have become keener.

LANGUAGE: VALUED PLURALISM AND MUTUAL IGNORANCE
Four National Languages

As mentioned, Switzerland has four national languages. Almost two-thirds of the population speak one of many Swiss-German dialects and, in meetings with other language communities or with foreigners, standard German. The three other national languages—French, Italian, and **Romansh**—belong to the **Romanic** family of languages. Their linguistic proximity to each other is closer than to German. The French speakers in Switzerland are also known as **Romands,** and the western region that they inhabit is the **Romandie.** Similarly, the **German-speaking** part has a name that goes back to one of the early Middle-Age tribes that settled there, **Alemannic Switzerland.**

The majority of the world's German, French, and Italian speakers, of course, live in the respective home countries of these languages—Germany, France, and Italy—who share common borders with Switzerland. To the east, two other countries, Austria and the tiny Principality of Liechtenstein, also are German-speaking. Romansh is spoken in Switzerland only. A considerable number of **immigrants** and some Swiss-born abroad speak a variety of other languages. The percentages for the various language groups are given in Table 2.

In contrast with some Americans, the Swiss appreciate the conviviality of several language groups. The concept of an educated person includes familiarity with one or several other languages. Schools try to live up to that demand: They "play a key role in bringing the languages closer together, for cantonal school regulations require that every child

TABLE 2

Language Communities

Language	Percent of Population
German	63.6
French	19.2
Italian	7.6
Romansh	0.6
Nonnational languages	8.9

Source: Federal Office of Statistics, "Eidgenössische Volkszählung 1990, Neue Vielfalt der Sprachen und Konfessionen der Schweiz," Press Release No. 31/93, Berne, May 1993.

learn a second national language from his or her seventh school year at the latest." (CCPSA 1993a: 1). Many Swiss credit themselves with a good command of at least one other national language and of English. Specific data were obtained from army recruits who were asked, in 1985, to rate their language skills. Considering that a person spoke a language "well" if it was the mother tongue or the person had had at least four years of training, no fewer than 85 percent of all young Swiss claimed to speak German well. Fifty percent checked French, 18 percent English and 6 percent Italian (Kreis 1993: 105).

And Will English Become the Fifth?

The figures speak to cultural ambitions and to the place of language instruction in schools but exaggerate the numbers of people with a good command of French and German. Two problems come together to create a gap between the cultural value of **multilingualism** and actual language proficiency.

First, the major language groups live in different territories: the French speakers in the west of Switzerland; those of Italian tongue on the southern slope of the Alps; the Germans in the east, the large Midlands, and some Alpine valleys. The Romansh are scattered to some small patches in the canton of Grisons. Few people grow up speaking more than one language in their families and immediate neighborhoods; of the recruits tested in 1985, about 4 percent were bilingual. Second, in their adult lives, a minority of the Swiss regularly face situations in which they must leap out of the comfort and security of their mother tongues. Kriesi et al. (1995b: 40) found that only one quarter of the people in Switzerland speak more than one national language in their normal daily lives.

The majority do not have that opportunity and tend to lose what skills they learned at school. As one would expect, the smaller a language community, the more often are its members obliged to express themselves in another language. Virtually all of the Romansh people also command German. Several surveys, however, have established that the Swiss-Germans have a better command of other national languages and of the English language than the French and Italian speakers (e.g., Kriesi et al. 1995b: 41). This has to do with the increasing insistence of Swiss-Germans, taken by anti-European reflexes, to speak their local dialects also in encounters with members of other language communities. When that is rejected, they would rather switch to French, Italian, or English than offer a standard German conversation. This weakens the incentive to study German. Except in Romansh country, youth in all language areas prefer to learn English rather than a Swiss national language as their second language, basically for professional reasons (Kreis 1993: 107). English may be on the way to becoming a lingua franca for intra-national communication in Switzerland.

We Get Along Well Because We Do Not Understand Each Other

The theory that Switzerland is a multilingual country living in peace and harmony because most of its citizens speak several of the national languages therefore has to be abandoned. The Swiss themselves have proposed a different explanation, one that is based on beneficial ignorance. They coined the saying "We get along well because we do not understand each other," first attributed to a president of the Confederation (Georges-André Chevallaz, *"Ils s'entendent bien, car ils ne se comprennent pas"*). Accordingly, most of life's affairs take place in one's own mother tongue, without interference from other language communities.

Even when the language communities seem to be speaking about the same subject, they may be approaching it through very different perspectives. For example, poverty in the 19th and early 20th centuries was so bad that the literati of all four national languages had no choice but to confront the plight of the poor. But the dominant preoccupations were not the same, as Camartin and others have shown (1992: 11–16). Key stories in German-speaking Switzerland gravitated around the moral depravity that economic ruin visited on small farmer and artisan families, or studied cycles of psychological depression in the poor. They debunked the myth of the virtuous poor and the religious merits of poverty. French-speaking novelists concentrated on the internal self-destructiveness of downwardly mobile genteel families. Italian- and Romansh-speaking Switzerland painted with a broader brush the tableau of entire economic classes in social change and the overturn of old values under the assault of the money economy. Here emigration and the illusions it nourished were popular themes: "In America, even the poorest have meat every day." Such images over time may have become fairly influential in their respective communities where generations of school children studied them in the textbooks of their 26 cantonal school systems, but they hardly transpired to other parts of Switzerland. A highbrow person in German-speaking Zurich if challenged on what French-speaking literature had to say on poverty might be tempted to show off with the great classics in France like Emile Zola's nineteenth-century novels, totally unaware of the native writers in western Switzerland. The public at large is even less likely to understand the outcroppings from different cultural traditions. For example, when French-speaking cantons objected to the government-supervised dispensation of methadone to drug addicts in Zurich, such policy divergencies were debated in contemporary moral and effectiveness terms. Little account was taken of the different cultural traditions. Among the German speakers, intellectuals had waged a long fight against self-righteousness and were therefore more accepting of certain forms of social deviance. In the Romandie, the belief of the French enlightenment that individuals could be perfected held sway. Such differences act on public policy, but the public may not always know the roots of tradition.

The language communities thus live in segmented spaces. The walls between them, paradoxically, have been made higher, not lower as we might expect, by the media revolution. It is, therefore, necessary to look at the relationship between the different media and the language communities.

The Media Reinforce Ties with Other Countries, and Weaken the Domestic Ones

Newspapers are the oldest mass media. The major papers all endeavor to have a fair news coverage, and admit opinion, from outside their own language areas. Their readership, however, is largely concentrated inside the areas: less than 1 in 10 readers lives in a different area, and of these few, many are migrants who wish to read a paper in their mother tongues. Most papers are local, and while they normally carry more stories from other regions and countries than local papers do in the United States, they have very few readers beyond their home districts. Moreover, newspapers predominantly interested in Swiss problems are no longer dominating the print media. In recent decades, a dazzling variety of magazines have come to fill the newsstands and kiosks, in large part produced in neighboring countries of the same language and, for technical subjects, in the United States. At the Geneva railway station, you may see an educated local walk out of the bookstore sporting the local *Journal de Genève* (Swiss, in French), *Le Monde Diplomatique* (from France) to bestow the aura of the Paris intellectual elite, as well as an American computer magazine. If, however, the person carries the *Neue Zürcher Zeitung" (Swiss, in German)* and *Der Spiegel* (from Germany), you would rather bet on a Swiss-German taking the train home to somewhere east of the Saane river.

While the Swiss newspapers, regardless of language, at least have editorial programs that keep a focus on the entire country and thereby reinforce national cohesion, the structure of the electronic media no longer lets us expect that effect. National public radio programs in four languages still command a share of 50 to 70 percent of the listenership. They suffer competition from private radios, whose outlook is far more local, and from foreign stations. The latter fill up to 30 percent of the time that the French-speaking minority spends listening to the radio. But it is television that has created the most fascinating consumer behavior, and the least favorable to dialogue between the language communities in Switzerland. For German-, French-, and Italian-speaking communities alike, between 60 and 70 percent of TV time goes for watching foreign programs, almost exclusively from the neighboring country of their own respective languages. National programs in the mother tongues make up between a quarter and a third of all TV consumption. A minute 2 to 5 percent of all TV time is devoted to watching Swiss programs in a language other than one's native idiom (Kriesi et al. 1995b: 45).

But the Political System Discourages Linguistic Antagonism

Those figures support the thesis of mutual ignorance among the language communities. It is the political system that makes sure, largely with success, that ignorance does not turn into antagonism. It buys language issues off, or breaks them down. In the Swiss scheme of local autonomy, it is the cantons who guarantee the traditional languages of their areas (Linder 1994: 22). National politics does not speak to local language questions, or indirectly only. Four cantons are special in that they are bilingual (Fribourg, Bern, and Valais: French/German) or trilingual (Grisons: German/Romansh/Italian). Here and in the federal polity, linguistic proportionality is well observed in personnel recruitment, in the composition of expert commissions, and for the chairs of legislative councils.

As a result, primary identification with one's language region is the exception rather than the rule. Many people identify first of all with their local **commune** or with their canton. But there are significant differences in the identification patterns on the dimensions near versus far, or small versus large. German speakers clearly distribute their affection between their home communes and Switzerland as a whole. The French speakers' identifications are more evenly spread out. Just as many feel they first of all are citizens of the world as there are localities, as Figure 2 shows.

Both groups relate most strongly to Switzerland as a nation (confirmed also by Melich 1991: 31). As far as the affection goes that the groups hold for each other, it appears the German speakers appreciate their Romand compatriots better than vice versa, a fact partially explained by the formers' superior foreign language skills. This leads to a cultural paradox: While the Romands have more trouble expressing themselves in other languages, they are universally credited with greater openness to the world, urbanity, and sophistication. It was customary, until modern vocational training opened new avenues at home, for young Swiss-German women to serve in a genteel Romand household to get a sense of this presumably

FIGURE 2

Language and Primary Identification Group

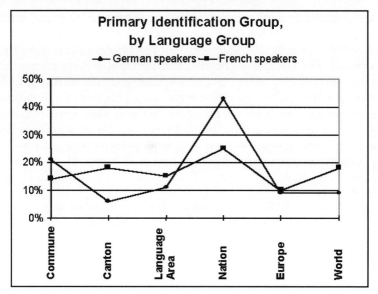

Source: Hanspeter Kriesi, Boris Wernli, Pascal Sciarini, and Mateo Gianni, "Le clivage linguistique: problèmes de Compréhension entre les communantés linguistiques en Suisses," Department of Political Science, University of Geneva, 1995, p. 107.

superior culture (the reverse movement, of young Romands apprenticing in German-speaking Switzerland, was virtually unknown). The paradox disappears when one takes into account the emotional relationship with Switzerland's neighbors. The Romands are generally attracted to their language mates, the French, and are in no small measure under the spell of Paris as a major cultural center. The feelings that the Swiss-Germans harbor about Germany are extremely ambivalent. The years of Hitler and the present-day economic weight of Germany have created emotional blockages behind which the Swiss-Germans are hiding in their dialects, folklore, and—increasingly dubious—satisfaction with Swiss business as usual.

Despite those differences, the mechanism for beneficial ignorance is shared by all the language communities: Inside their segmented spaces, yet smaller units—cantons and communes—exercise the autonomy of the federalist state. Across boundaries, dialogue is sustained by the substantial (although not overwhelmingly high) number of multilingual speakers. The Confederation finally recognizes the national languages and ensures their appropriate political and cultural representation. This tripartite recipe—local autonomy, multilingual orientation, federal support—has been largely successful over the 150-year course of modern Switzerland. Its success was possible because the boundaries of the language regions remained remarkably stable over time. No one felt threatened by the other groups' demographic advance.

Agreement—Most of the Time

But the Swiss multilingual conviviality has known periods of strain as well, and many observers believe that the country is entering a period of greater conflict on those lines again. The strain comes from two sources: from perceived domestic inequity as well as from the "strong cultural links . . . that the country . . . entertains with neighboring regions. These relationships are somewhat ambivalent as they vary historically between a strong leaning towards a neighboring culture and a rejection of it because it appears to pose a threat to Swiss identity" (CCPSA 1993a: 1). A major challenge for the national unity was created by the antagonism between France and Germany, more generally by the cultural struggle between Germanic and Romanic peoples that led up to the First World War. Switzerland was deeply divided in her sympathies with the warring parties, and the rift between its polarized language communities was dislodged only by a deeper one, the class struggle of the twenties and thirties. Conversely, the Second World War united all groups against the fascist threat. In the years of strong economic growth that followed, all communities participated, and the antagonisms between surrounding countries were subdued in the Cold War. Harmony prevailed in Switzerland. The erosion of old values in those years brought the language question back into the political arena in the mid-60s, that is, long before economic growth slowed down, but the temperatures always remained mild. Voter research allows us to quantify the degree of dissension: Between 1972 and 1992, 163 federal ballots were voted. The French-speaking areas decided differently from the German-speaking cantons in 29 ballots, or 18 percent of all events. In four-fifths of all ballot-worthy questions, the two largest language communities were in agreement.

Yet total figures say nothing about which issues are particularly important and about the conditions that cause the language community to disagree most vehemently. After Switzerland entered a period of slow economic growth in 1974, the costs were not uniformly borne by all the regions. The Romanic areas were saddled with unemployment rates double or higher than those in German-speaking Switzerland. In particular, the French-speaking community began to look to the European Community for economic revitalization.

French Speakers Are More Open to Europe

When public arenas are so deeply segmented, deliberations of important national issues can get out of sync between the language groups. In recent years, that has happened. Chiefly it has been foreign policy issues that have driven a wedge between the language communities. In 1986, the Swiss people rejected adhesion to the **United Nations.** In 1992, in what many consider the most important proposition of this century brought before popular ballot, the people kept the country out of the **European Economic Area.**

Opposition to the United Nations was inspired by concern for Swiss neutrality in view of the (then still-active) East–West and other conflicts. The European Economic Area was a massive pork barrel issue. In particular, the large domestically oriented sector of the economy feared it would lose out to foreign competition if protective barriers were pulled down. Beyond that, concern for the future of the Swiss model of **direct democracy** was vivid. The campaign was loud and bitter, voter turnout was high (78.3 percent), and the outcome was very narrow, with 50.3 percent voting against it. Along what lines were the Swiss people divided in an issue so consequential for their future?

Vatter (1994), in a study of the voting behavior of over 1,800 communes, showed that language, moderately significant in the United Nations vote in 1986, advanced to explain nearly three-quarters of the differences in 1992. This study warrants brief summary here because it allows us to gauge the strength of different factors. For the European Economic Area vote, the influence of four types of factors on the outcome were compared. At first, Vatter estimated the influence of each of them in isolation. Cultural factors—language and religion—accounted for 69 percent of the differences. Socio-structural variables—education and income levels of communes, peripheral versus central location, age structure, and unemployment levels—were less than half as influential (29 percent), closely followed by the strength of political affiliations (28 percent). The local economy determined the outcome to a small degree only (5 percent), with the strongest pressure being exerted by the share of farming in employment.

Vatter then ran a more demanding model that estimated the influence of the four factors jointly. Together, they accounted for 85 percent of the voting differences. In this model, the strength of the cultural factor is even stronger; the influence of the French language is six times as great as the second strongest indicator, which is the share of the **right**-wing party that led the opposition to Switzerland going European. The structure of the economy is virtually irrelevant as a direct factor. Its influence is almost entirely mediated through other factors.

The implication is that economic factors such as higher unemployment may initially have created a disposition for the French speakers to be more open to the European Economic Area. But the economic differences between the regions were not important enough to produce the vast differences in the vote. It took the cultural factor to blow them up to this point: In the run-up to the ballot, deliberations were caught up in public spaces distinctly separated between the language groups. On each side, majority opinions grew stronger and stronger as the ballot day approached. Opinions spiraled in opposite directions because the voters were little exposed to voices from the other language communities.

A New Rift: Cosmopolitans versus Traditionalists

Vatter's unit of study was the smallest collectivity for which he had European Economic Area voting data, the commune. Kriesi, Longchamps, and others (1993) followed individual voters. They found another important cultural dimension besides language but partly linked to it. This concerns the opposition between winners and losers of the modernization process in Switzerland. Many of the winners feel strong enough to live in a united Europe, while all but a few of the losers look backward to a past in which the country's high borders and the solidarity of the small town secured their social positions. In the European Economic Area debate, the federal government strongly recommended for Switzerland to join Europe. For that lack of neutrality, **traditionalists** expressed strong distrust in the government. Kriesi and others therefore investigated the influence of language, city versus country, and, as a measure of traditionalism, mistrust in the government. They found that confidence in the government had a much stronger effect than language or location. But that factor interacted with the language communities and the urban-rural difference. Only 44 percent of the interviewees said they trusted the authorities in this issue. Most of those who mistrusted lived in the German-speaking majority region. Their big number eventually swung the vote to the negative. The decisive influence of this group is clearly visible in Figure 3, which gives the strength of the yes vote for each of the eight subgroups formed.

FIGURE 3

Dimensions of Openness to Europe

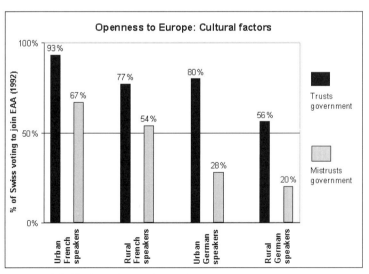

Source: Reconstructed after Kriesi, Longchamp, et al. 1993: 39.

Kriesi's findings are significant in as much as they confirm that the opposition between **cosmopolitan** and **traditionalist** elements has established itself as a new political and cultural dimension in Switzerland. In the European Economic Area issue, that went hand in hand with the language distinctions. Ever since, the Swiss have worried about a growing estrangement between the Romandie and the rest of the country.

MODERN DEVELOPMENTS: CHANGE ITSELF IS CHANGING

Belated Autonomy of the Individual

One of my early reading favorites from the parish library was the story of a poor child sent away because his parents could not feed him. A city boy, he is reluctantly admitted to a farm family who are poor themselves. Unfit to help with the chores, he gets beaten up by the farmer. Friends from the village school hide him in the haystack of another farm until benevolent adults—the commune president, the policeman, and a wealthy widow—work out a better living arrangement. The thrill was all about the hide-and-seek game between the young conspirators and the adults who had the final charge, but the moral of the book was that village life, despite the rare bad guy and the hard work, was healthier and friendlier than the city (which we never meet in the book).

Before 1970, the story was typical of what Swiss youth would read. Analyses of school textbooks, youth literature, and historical novels have shown that the objectives of basic education changed only minimally for more than 150 years (Kreis 1993: 67–69). The world for which children were prepared existed less and less in reality. The Alpine landscape was painted large as the seat of liberty. Women were not prominent (the widow in the book was an exception, needed in the role of unselfish helper). The repertoire of modern roles was minimal, featuring again and again the same famous railway engineers. Henry Dunant, the founder of the Red Cross, received his due place in education as an example of Swiss international charity, but the economic and political conflicts that led to the wars mobilizing the Red Cross were barred from curricula. Strangers were depicted negatively (which was disingenuous for a country that earned a lot of money from foreign tourists). Popular novels for adults also cultivated an orientation to the past. They taught conformity, modesty, and nature adoration (the latter at least opened a niche for women, together with hiking and singing groups). When in the 1930s urban themes eventually made an entry, they were immediately balanced with mythical mountain novels. The anxieties and the national unity appeals during the Hitler reign in Germany (1933–45) gave another lease on life to what had become a straight-jacket cultural order. Paradoxically, it was in the fifties, when the majority of the Swiss realized they were no longer living in poverty, that the country gradually became saddled with self-doubt. By 1970, economic transformation, the student rebellion, and the Vietnam war opened up Switzerland for a more liberal culture.

We are dealing with cultural modernization that proceeded more slowly than in neighboring countries. Switzerland was late in acknowledging the autonomy of the individual in the conduct and regulation of modern life. For example, the private sphere became a legitimate subject of public media only in the sixties. In Germany and Austria, however, a tabloid press thriving on human interest stories of the common man had been strong since the interwar period. The political enfranchisement of the Swiss women, which only took place in 1971, and the spying by the federal police into the political leanings of 100,000 citizens (also culminating in the early seventies), are other indicators of a culture retarded by authoritarian traditionalism.

Faster Pace after 1970

Since 1970, however, Switzerland has followed most cultural developments of other advanced nations such as the media revolution and the sexual revolution and international tourism. Differences with other western countries seem to be minor. But two overarching results of recent cultural change are crystallizing out: One concerns the growing polarity between those who are open toward the larger world and those who are more inward-looking. The other is a keener awareness of the speed of cultural and social change.

Not all the Swiss people are equally approving of the changes. Many deplore the loss of what to them seem to be unique and valuable characteristics of Swiss life. While Switzerland lowered her barriers with the outside world, cultural differences within the country have widened. Increasingly, these differences are expressed also in the political arena. As analyzed earlier, the European Economic Area vote in 1992 was the most dramatic battle in this struggle so far. With the continuing worldwide economic changes challenging Switzerland, the cultural polarity is set to become sharper. As more of the traditional structures dissolve, their defense, and where possible artificial recreation, will mobilize **conservative** forces. Sometimes small vignettes can illustrate that best: Never in recent decades have small farmers been so badly beleaguered as they are now, and never before has the cow as a symbol of Swiss culture been so aggressively marketed on all sorts of objects. It is as though the farmers pleaded to be safeguarded in a museum just before disappearing under the assault of the market.

Regardless of individual preferences for the direction and results of cultural change, a consensus has formed on the assumption that it has accelerated. It is not the simple fact that something is changing, but it is the change of the change itself that attracts attention. For example, the generation that grew up in the sixties and the seventies knew that they had greater freedom to choose their professions than their parents did. Many did in fact change careers once or several times during their lifetime. Much more recent is the awareness that one may *have* to change, and that life-long work becomes lifelong learning.

One Culture, or Many Cultures?

For the Swiss, the 1990 census results were an eye-opener. Between 1980 and 1990, most of the population increase, it was found, came from immigrants. Immigrants established new linguistic and religious minorities. The Swiss, for their part, reached new levels of individualization, with its potential for greater cultural diversity. They are struggling to understand the new situation. Inflationary use is made of labels like **"multicultural"** and "mobile" before the facts, let alone the implications, are properly understood. Not surprisingly, in a state that takes an active role in defining the national culture, official pronouncements chime in with the chorus of multiculturalism. Thus, the Federal Office of Statistics states that "Switzerland is in the process of becoming a multicultural society" although "it is still necessary to analyze and clarify the causes and links" among its major characteristics (1994b: 1). Hoffmann-Nowotny (1996: 6) has suspected that the breakdown of communism has left an ideological void everywhere, including in Swiss public debates. With no workers' class left to bid for political power, group rights based on ethnic minorities will increasingly be advanced, to compete with the classic concept of individual rights. If his prediction is true, it will create similarities with affirmative action debates in the United States. Perhaps in order to forestall that, Swiss immigration policy is being reviewed in ways that may end up preferring immigrants from nearby European countries.

But nobody knows if managed multiculturalism is feasible. At the 1996 Olympic games, a gold medal for Switzerland was won by a man of Chinese extraction. Meanwhile, in Zurich, a right-wing party section tried to thwart the establishment of a **Muslim** cemetery, obliging families to bury their dead as far away as Turkey. Despite preoccupations with the economy, the fight for the future of Swiss culture is not going to be subdued.

SOCIAL INEQUALITY: CLOSER TO THE UNITED STATES THAN TO GERMANY AND JAPAN

Inequality—Even the Government Says So

After looking at some of the constant points as well as paradoxes of Swiss culture, we now turn to the second mainstay of society—social structure understood as an ordered system of social positions. What is of particular interest here, notably for the reader who wishes to compare with the US situation, is the extent to which Swiss social structure gives individuals unequal access to the means of sustenance and personal fulfillment.

In Switzerland, critics do not carry a heavy burden of proof for their theories of inequality. The federal government itself recognizes the very unequal character of Swiss society. The official view is that "wealth is very unequally distributed within the country," and that "social inequality has tended to increase . . . in recent years" (with the exception of education; CCPSA, 1993c: 2). In a country that has incorporated **socialist** parties in government for so long, such candor is hardly surprising. But it stops at admitting a broad notion. While the trend toward greater inequality is commonly deplored, few Swiss have a more precise idea of its extent. International income comparisons rank the country among the Western nations with more pronounced income disparities, much closer to the United States than to neighboring Germany (or, for that matter, to Japan, with its even narrower gap). Table 3 uses the income ratio between the 20 percent richest and the 20 percent poorest members of society as a point of comparison.

While many of the rich Swiss thrive on investment returns, the majority of the people depend on wages and salaries for their livelihood. It is, therefore, necessary to see the **stratification** of positions in the professional realm. Of the 6.87 million residents counted in 1990, 3.58 million, or 52 percent, were working outside of their household and training jobs. The census used a set of eight socioprofessional categories that combine to form a nearly hierarchical scale. The (rounded) percentages of the working population that belong to the different categories are shown in Table 4.

TABLE 3

Comparative Income Inequality

Country	Income Inequality (20% richest versus 20% poorest households)
Japan	4.2
Sweden	4.6
Netherlands	5.6
Germany	5.7
Switzerland	8.5
United States	9.1

Source: Beat Hotz-Hart, Stefan Maeder, and Patrick Vock, *Volkswirtschaft der Schweiz* (Zurich: vdf Hochschulverlag AG an der ETH Zurich, 1995), p. 307. Data are for 1980. Kerbo (1996: 29), however, gives a ratio of 12 for the United States.

TABLE 4

Swiss Social Classes by Socioprofessional Status, in 1990

Socioprofessional Category	Percent in Gainful Employment
Top management	1%
Classical professions (doctors, lawyers, clergy)	1
Self-employed	10
Academic professions and upper management	9
Middle employees	20
Skilled nonmanual professions	24
Skilled manual professions	13
Unskilled manual workers and employees	23

Source: Federal Office of Statistics, "Eidgenössische Volkszählung 1990: Ein Blick in die Sozialstruktur der Schweiz," Pressemitteilung No. 71/95, Berne, November 1995, p. 4.

The Focus on the Middle Class Disguises a Runaway Elite

At first glance, the percentages suggest a neat three-class system, confirming the everyday experience of a broad middle class. The four upper layers, charged with directing organizations and public belief systems, make up roughly 20 percent of the total. The lower class, formed of the unskilled, would also count for one-fifth of the active population. In this 20/60/20 scheme, the most important boundaries of socioprofessional groups correspond to the quintiles used in income comparisons. But such a classification is in itself tarnished with a middle-class outlook. Switzerland is as yet deficient in studies of those who through unemployment and other hazards have become chronically marginal. Research on the poor, the unemployed, and others not fitting any of the professional categories (e.g., retirees) is new and not much integrated with classical stratification research. On the top of the system, the powerful political and economic elites are also not adequately discerned by the broad classifications (Kerbo 1996: 14, 335). Kriesi (1980) has shown how closely knit and small the political elite are in Switzerland. I know of no similar study of the economic elite.

However, income studies based on tax records draw a daunting picture when the top and bottom *10 percent* are compared. A long-term view is necessary. The relative distance, as far as *incomes* are concerned, was largely unaltered in the first half of the century, a period of slow growth. After the riches speculators accumulated during World War II were gone, the ratio between the top and bottom shares picked up exactly at its prewar value of 5:1. But then, obscured by the widespread growth of incomes during the Golden Thirty Years, 1945 to 1975, the gap climbed with almost constant force. After a brief lull in the second half of the sixties, it reached the 13:1 mark in 1993 (Levy et al. 1997: Ch. 4, p. 47). The distribution of *assets* has gone to even more staggering extremes. The net worth of the highest and lowest deciles stood at 22:1 in 1958; by 1993, this figure had soared to an unbelievable 274 :1 (Levy et al. 1997: Ch. 4, p. 48).

I do not have comparable time series for aggregate income shares in the United States and Switzerland. In 1990, the top 20 percent earners in both countries scored surprisingly similar portions, around 45 percent (Kerbo 1996: 23; Hotz-Hart et al. 1995: 526). It is indubitable that over the last 20 years social inequality has increased in both countries. Prior to that, they knew periods during which the inequality was slightly reversed or at least kept constant. There is some evidence (Levy et al. 1997: Ch. 4, pp. 47–48) that this happened in Switzerland later and only for a shorter time. It is a matter of speculation whether greater equality, together with higher average incomes, expanded education, and the baby boom, were responsible for the cultural revolution that transformed Western countries in the 60s. If that is the case, it might help explain why this change was particularly late and tepid in Switzerland. Another major difference is the presence of a large group of foreigners in the lower class in Switzerland. If only Swiss incomes and wealth are considered, the spread will be narrower than in the United States.

SOCIAL MOBILITY: A COLLECTIVE ASCENDANCY HALTED

The Levy Elevator

The 1990 distribution of people over the socioprofessional categories is a one-point-in-time snapshot of Swiss society. How did the Swiss get there? Well, they took the Levy Elevator. In 1950, there were about 900,000 Swiss and 150,000 foreign workers. The higher-placed employees were in much smaller numbers, some 300,000 Swiss and only a few thousand foreigners. By 1970, when the number of foreign workers was at its maximum, the number of Swiss workers had fallen to 800,000 and the ranks of foreigners had multiplied to 500,000 workers. Among the Swiss, 800,000 now counted themselves as employees. The higher and top management sections were populated with double the number of Swiss than in 1950 as well as a small number of foreigners. Not only was the elevator thus used to transport more people (more Swiss, more immigrants, more jobs), but it also carried more of them to higher floors. The occupational structure continued to change over the next 20 years, but less dramatically so. A series of recessions starting in the mid-seventies and accelerated structural change of the economy after 1985 hit both Swiss and foreigners. Several hundred thousand foreigners left the country in the seventies, buffering the Swiss against unemployment. They returned together with job growth in the eighties. Since then, enterprise restructurings and lean management concepts have put pressure on employee and middle-management positions.

Two Kinds of Mobility:
Structural and Circulation

Swiss society obviously underwent a great deal of what sociologists call "structural mobility"—movements into social positions that are created by the changes in the occupational structure. By far the most radical change came through immigration and the large share that foreigners came to fill of the lower-end jobs. The sociologist Hoffmann-Nowotny (Levy et al. 1997: Ch. 4, p. 41) coined the German term *Unterschichtung* for the process that took place chiefly between 1950 and 1970. An ambiguous concept defying literal translation, it means both the broadening of the low ranks of stratification and the laying of a foundation (of gravel or concrete) under an existing house. The implication is that the Swiss house was lifted up in the process. The foreign workforce allowed a large number of Swiss to advance to the middle class. This strong center is a cornerstone of modern Swiss society. It is being put under pressure by recent changes, but has not been dislodged.

The importance of the middle class does not guarantee stable positions for all of its members. In fact, when we look at the family and individual careers of this group in Switzerland, we find that they circulate much faster than people at the top or bottom of the social ladder. Levy and his group took several indicators of "circulation mobility." This is the part of the changes between positions that would occur even if the occupational structure stayed fixed. In the classical manner of mobility studies, they divided their investigation between aspects of intergenerational and intragenerational **social mobility.** The first refers to changes between the individual's social position and that of his or her parents. The second looks at the changes undergone in one's own lifetime.

So, how many people do change positions between generations? Fortunately, we also have data from the United States. Table 5 gives percentages of those who stay in the same class as their parents. The first label is the one used by Levy et al. (1997), followed by the terms used in the American study. They are substantively equivalent.[1]

The Middle Class Is Mobile, but Less
Than in the United States

The strongest impressions one gets from Table 5 is that mobility out of the middle class in Switzerland is much weaker than in the United States. At the lower end, conversely, American workers find it harder to rise to the middle class over generations. But also for unskilled workers

---

1. I have used their data as well as data provided for the United States. The US data is from a study that Western and Wright (1994) conducted on the permeability of class boundaries in several countries. Their scheme of socioprofessional categories has influenced the one used by Levy et al (1997), which was designed to be comparable although the wording of the group terms is different.

TABLE 5

Intergenerational Hereditarity

Socioprofessional Category	Switzerland	United States
Top management/Employers	17%*	18%
Academic professions and upper management/ Expert managers	51	28
Middle employees/Managers	43	13
Classical professions and other self-employed/ Petty bourgeoisie	26	10
Skilled nonmanual professions/Professionals	24	12
Skilled manual professions/Semiprofessionals	16	11
Unskilled manual workers and employees/Workers	31	52

*Share of those who stayed in the same class from parent to respondent.

Sources: René Levy, Dominique Joye, Olivier Guye, and Vincent Kaufmann, "Tous égaux en Suisse? De la stratification aux représentations," Lausanne, 1997, Ch. 15, p. 21; and Mark Western and Erik Olin Wright, "The Permeability of Class Boundaries to Intergenerational Mobility among Men in the United States, Canada, Norway, and Sweden," *American Sociological Review* 59 (August 1994), p. 626.

in Switzerland, intergenerational permanency is a fate much more often encountered than for their skilled colleagues. Many of the children of unskilled foreign workers find themselves caught on the bottom.

On the top, interpretation of the figures needs some additional information. With a low 17 percent (18 percent for the United States), families in the topmost class do not seem to be capable of holding on to their positions over time in either country. But when we also consider the flows between top management and the upper-management echelons, it is clear that these two top groups are sustaining each other in large measure. Recruitment from lower down is a minority event for the upper class in both countries. When it does happen, the Swiss upper class seems to be taking in preferentially offspring of middle managers; in the US upper class, more children arrive from worker and self-employed families.

Both studies have investigated the barriers that prevent the generations from moving to a different class. Three kinds of resources that help to overcome barriers were examined: property of the means of production, authority acquired by hierarchical position in organizations, and expertise gained from education and training. Interestingly, the barriers to mobility in Switzerland and the United States are very different. Authority does not seem, or no longer seems, to make class boundaries impervious. Property, however, is a fortress wall around the upper class that Americans find much more difficult to overcome than the Swiss do. In Switzerland, the hardest barrier seems to be erected by the education factor. The crucial importance of formal education for getting ahead in life is a trait that Switzerland shares with other Germanic countries and also with Sweden.

What happened to the system over time? Some forms of analysis, notably comparisons between 10-year cohorts, can be employed to follow changes. The findings of Levy's group in this respect are rather sobering. In Switzerland, despite structural changes in the economy, the character of mobility barriers has hardly changed (Levy et al. 1997: Ch. 5, p. 45). But remember that their figures include both Swiss citizens and foreigners. The ones in the middle who enjoy more mobility are largely the Swiss, many of whom arrived there through structural mobility processes. Moreover, by lumping together some of the socioprofessional categories into three classes, we would find that the proportion of immobiles between generations is roughly between 30 and 40 percent. This figure is similar to that found for Britain and France (Erikson and Goldthorpe 1993). For the extent of intergenerational fluidity, Switzerland apparently is not much different from other European societies.

A New Sight: Downwardly Mobile Swiss

With low levels of economic growth, faster structural change, and higher unemployment, the Swiss of the nineties have woken up to a new sight: downward social mobility in their own ranks. Loss of status and income nowadays happens more frequently within one's lifetime; we are therefore speaking of an *intra*generational phenomenon. Two factors have created awareness that lately there have been more people on downward elevator trips: First, the affected groups changed. Before 1980, occupational descent disproportionately often hit foreign women. In the eighties, the Swiss also became exposed, although the women more than the men (Buchmann et al. 1996: 47). In the nineties, restructurings of big employers such as the major Swiss banks demonstrate the fragility of middle-class positions. Second, intragenerational vertical mobility in Switzerland has traditionally been less pronounced than in other countries such as the United States or even its neighbors France and Austria (Levy et al. 1997: Ch. 5, pp. 5–7). Although this is nowhere explicitly stated, probably the greater importance of education for status attainment is a leading cause for low mobility. At the end of their education, the Swiss seem to be launched on career paths that are predetermined by their education certificates, and therefore rarely undergo dramatic status changes between the ages of 25 and 45.

Between those two ages the vertically mobile are found primarily among those who change careers. Even there they do not exceed 30 percent. The immobility of those who stay in their professional lines is massive: Only 8 percent of those faithful to their professions experience a change of status at all. The percentages of the downwardly mobile were therefore very modest until 1990, estimated by Buchmann and others to be around 2.8 percent over all groups (up from 1.4 percent before 1980). By that time, the importance of upward mobility was almost exactly the same, indicating that there was little room for structural vertical mobility left in the 90s.

Horizontally, the changes are more important. The economy forces greater occupational flexibility. More people nowadays change career paths, and these reorientations often take place early in life. In 1990, half of all working persons in the age group 25–34 years were no longer working in the profession for which they had been trained. It hardly concurs with traditional images of practicing one's learned profession all life long.

But Most Adults Still Live in Fairly Stable Conditions

In sum, what is striking about Switzerland is the fact that vertical mobility seems to be much stronger *between* generations than *within* recent generations. The Swiss are used to definite changes of status between parents and children, certainly in the middle class. At the same time, the individuals have been able to count on relatively settled conditions in their own adult lives. This is changing now, in a situation of growing social inequality. The indicators extant (until 1990) show that clearly, but do not speak of dramatic changes. In fact, employers complain that occupational flexibility is not keeping pace with the dynamics of the international marketplace (Hotz-Hart et al. 1995: 308). While the changes are slow, the outside pressures make for a consistent momentum. It is likely that mobility rates as well as wealth and income disparities will grow further.

WOMEN: FLYING WITH WINGS OF WAX

Slow Access to Modern Institutions

The kinds of stratification and income research on which the previous section drew mostly look at the situation of the main breadwinner in a family. As such, they say little about the female half of the population because only a minority of women are in that category. More fundamental measures, therefore, are needed that determine access to institutions even before measuring positions and rewards.

Such an approach is still pertinent for the situation of Swiss women. They have acceded to several of the modern institutional realms more slowly than their peers of other industrial countries. The best publicized historical lag concerned the right to vote, which women received only in 1971, 51 years after it had come to American women. Various participation rates speak to the persistence of traditional division of **gender** roles and to a degree of discrimination that is more pronounced than in other countries of comparable wealth. In 1993, the United Nations, in one of its periodic worldwide quality-of-life surveys, used an index that combined income, wealth, employment, education,

FIGURE 4

Female Participation in Various Institutions

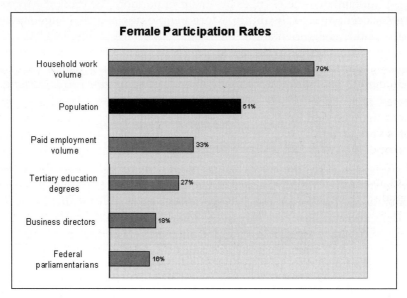

Female Participation Rates

- Household work volume — 79%
- Population — 51%
- Paid employment volume — 33%
- Tertiary education degrees — 27%
- Business directors — 18%
- Federal parliamentarians — 16%

Sources: Calculated from various works cited in the text.

and health data on both sexes. This Human Development Index allows measurement of the difference in the quality of life between men and women. Countries then are ranked according to the relative position of women. The first four places all went to Scandinavian countries. Neither the United States (rank 13) nor Switzerland (rank 19) belonged to the leading group. But they did better than two of East Asia's industrial nations, Japan (21) and South Korea (33) (Kerbo 1996: 302). The gender gap in human development in Switzerland was about one and a half of the American differential.

Swiss data confirm the importance of the gap, also for institutional areas that the United Nations index did not cover. Figure 4 visualizes the extremes. Consonant with the strength of traditional female roles, Swiss women do four-fifths of all work in the household. At the top of the business and political decision making, the rates are reversed; it is men who take four-fifths of the seats in directors' offices and in the **Federal Assembly.**

Fewer Women Are Employed
Than in the United States

The indicators with medium values—labor market participation and education—are the ones on which some recent historical data are available. Over the two decades from 1967 to 1987, women of most advanced countries have entered the labor market in ever-increasing numbers. Japan and Ireland were the rare exceptions with female participation rates remaining practically constant. If one goes by the OECD figures (OECD 1991: 131), Switzerland remained static until 1986. Since then more women have found work, particularly part-time work.

What is striking, however, is a clear tendency toward regional clusters. The Scandinavian countries again form the top league, with female labor rates between 70 and 80 percent. In Canada and the United States, almost exactly two-thirds of the women were in paid employment in 1987. Those six countries expanded their female participation rates very fast, by up to 25 percent. Five contiguous countries in central Europe—France, Switzerland, Austria, Germany, and Belgium—crowded into a narrow band between 51 and 54 percent. Several countries in southern Europe—Greece, Italy, and Spain—have expanded female participation faster than the central European countries, but they started from a much lower base and therefore are still at lower levels. These distinct regional similarities suggest that women's access to paid work has largely been determined by cultural factors. In Switzerland, conservative attitudes regarding women's enrollment were for a long time firmed up by structural factors. The country had not participated in the war; therefore, there was no male demographic gap to be filled. Cheap foreign labor became available after the war. Essentially, what needs to be retained here is the fact that fewer women work outside the household than in the United States.

A Scarcity of Full-Time Jobs and Senior Positions

At first, we need to look at the type of work that women do in Switzerland. Women make up 43 percent of all persons employed, but because many held part-time or minimal employment in 1990, they supplied only one-third of the total work volume (Federal Office of Statistics, 1993a: 51). In fact, three-quarters of all full-time jobs were held by men and over four-fifths of all part-time work was done by women.

The relative scarcity of full-time jobs for women has repercussions on their hierarchical positions in the economy (see Table 6). We have already noted the 1:5 gender ratio for directors. Women are clearly a minority also among employees who supervise others. They are at almost equal numbers with men at the operative level, dominate clearly among workers who contribute to a family business, but hold less than two-fifths of all apprenticeship contracts.

With women being concentrated in the lower ranks of employment, we expect to find lower average pay. This is the case, although not as extreme as in the United States. On average, Swiss women bring home hourly wages that are 28 percent lower than those for men (Federal Office of Statistics, 1993a: 64). The US figure, for full-time, year-round workers in 1986, was 35 percent lower than for men (Schaefer and Lamm

TABLE 6

Women and Hierarchical Positions in the Economy

Status Level	Female Share
Directors	18%
Employees in supervisory role	29
Employees without supervisory function	51
Contributing to family business	72
Self-employed	29
Apprentices	36

Source: Federal Office of Statistics, *Auf dem Wege zur Gleichstellung? Frauen und Männer in der Schweiz aus statistischer Sicht* (Berne: Federal Office of Statistics, 1993), p. 55.

1989: 232). In Switzerland, about half of the difference is explained by human-capital factors: women's lower education or job experience. The other half is due to **ascriptive factors:** the difference in pay that persists when human-capital factors are the same for men and women. This is the amount of direct income discrimination that Swiss women suffer (Brüderl et al. 1993: 584).

Schoolchildren Come Home for Lunch

The indirect discrimination, based on limited access to human capital, is also considerable. We shall address the education situation in a moment. Job experience is interrupted, and then devalued, by the family and child-rearing cycle. Among women without children under the age of 15, 56 percent are employed full time; while they raise children, only 20 percent pursue full-time employment (Federal Office of Statistics, 1993a: 53). A number of structural arrangements help explain the low participation of mothers: Child-care arrangements are scarce; schoolchildren return home for two-hour lunchbreaks; and, at least into the eighties, because male wages were high, it was possible for most Swiss families to raise a family on a single income (Charles and Buchman 1994: 599).

A report by the Federal Commission for Women's Issues summarized the labor participation for the past 15 years: "The Swiss women have made good quantitatively but without any qualitative improvement of the situation" (1995: 137). What are the causes of the enduring discrimination? Three layers of causation can be evoked: the recruitment into jobs, access to education, and the ambient culture with its role typifications for women.

TABLE 7

Gender Domination in Employment

	Branch	Female Share of Employment, 1991
Male-dominated	Construction	2%
	Technical Professions	13
Integrated	Agriculture and Animal Husbandry	34
	Sales	60
Female-dominated	Hospitality	79
	Health Care	80

Source: Federal Office of Statistics, *Auf dem Wege zur Gleichstellung? Frauen und Männer in der Schweiz aus statistischer Sicht* (Berne: Federal Office of Statistics, 1993), p. 60.

Occupations Highly Segregated by Sex

Occupations in Switzerland are highly sex segregated. Charles and Buchman (1994) calculated a sex-segregation index for 25 industrial countries and found that Switzerland's level of segregation was surpassed only by one other country: Luxembourg. Women are overrepresented in clerical, sales, and service occupations. Men predominate in managerial and manufacturing jobs. Table 7 gives examples of male- (<30 percent) and female-dominated (>70 percent) employment as well as integrated branches.

The job market for women is compressed into a smaller number of occupations than are available for men. Just four occupations account for half of all female employment, and all four are in the service sector. It takes the 10 most important occupations to absorb half the male workforce (Federal Office of Statistics, 1993a: 58–59). Moreover, women who have been trained in female-dominated occupations hardly ever switch to **integrated** or male-dominant branches. This is true even of those women who change occupation. Having children strengthens the bond to the female-dominated sector of occupation. A woman with a completed university education and a mother with post-secondary education can open the door to the other sectors, but only by a very small measure (Charles and Buchman 1994: 611–614). Sex-typing and occupation-specific credentials have strong long-range effects on opportunities in Switzerland.

Segregation Also in Academic Fields

That takes us back to the point about education and class barriers. As mentioned earlier, Switzerland is one of those Germanic countries in which education erects particularly high barriers to upward mobility.

TABLE 8

Gender Domination in Academic Disciplines

	Discipline	Women among Graduates 1990
Male-dominated	Exact sciences	9%
	Engineering	15
	Economics and business	21
Integrated	Medicine	41
	Social sciences	59
	Humanities	63

Source: Federal Office of Statistics, *Auf dem Wege zur Gleichstellung? Frauen und Männer in der Schweiz aus statistischer Sicht* (Berne: Federal Office of Statistics, 1993), p. 43.

Here the Swiss women have made great historic advances over the past two generations. Those women who had only the mandatory years of education decreased from a majority to under one-fifth, and the gender gap was reduced greatly.

The progress has been countered by the cost of certificate inflation in the job market. Tertiary-level education thus becomes increasingly critical for upward mobility. At this level, too, women have made impressive gains. Men seem to have leveled out, with, in 1990, about double the number of university graduations relative to women. However, similarly to sex-typing in vocational training, academic disciplines have undergone very contrasting degrees of feminization. The more a discipline is regarded as "soft science," the higher the share of women graduates. Table 8 lists male-dominated and integrated branches using the same breakpoints as for occupational dominance. Note, however, that there are no clearly female-dominated academic disciplines.

It is debatable that human capital factors are just as much responsible as cultural factors for wage and mobility differentials. But the strong affinity between the sexes and academic disciplines seems to be an outcome purely of culture, particularly childhood socialization. Women, in its crudest formulation, are more attracted to social tasks; men, more to technology. What the graduation statistics show is confirmed by data from altogether different realms.

Men and Women Combine Their Engagements Differently

In Switzerland as elsewhere, the segregation between family life and other spheres has decreased, but the way the two sexes combine activities in the different fields varies widely. Men center their lives around their professions; women, more around their families. These poles of life are surrounded by institutional participations that form gender-specific clusters. Men find political activities, engagement in professional associations, and marriage mutually reinforcing. For women, family is made to be a value in itself, not so much a resource for other institutional participations. Likewise the effort that women invest in professional associations is related more closely with an actual employment role and not with political activism. Voluntary associations and politics form another cluster for both men and women, but for women service in these associations is often complemented with yet other engagements in the **churches,** a relationship from which men are absent (Levy et al. 1997: Ch. 7, pp. 8–11).

Informal groups, voluntary associations, and local radio have created important social spaces reserved for women. These arenas, often overlooked, build bridges between women isolated in traditional family roles and the public. They help women cope with familial and job conflicts. Not too rare are the Swiss housewives doing chores accompanied by the local radio talkmaster, where they can phone in; and then switching over to the ideologically more correct public radio the very moment the husband is heard driving into the garage.

A Waste of Talent

The limited and belated response to the Swiss women's aspirations has veered between the ridiculous and the tragic. Men made fools of themselves, for example, when they insisted for 40 years, from the inception of the women's national athletics day in 1932 until the sixties' cultural revolution, that women could not organize this event. Only when women took over the direction of the committee in 1972 was competitive gymnastics released from the stigma "unnatural for women" (Kreis 1993: 159). Women who rebelled too bravely against their constricted situation were occasionally ostracized or had to find creative outlets in exile. The waste of talent under the strictures of tradition is the subject of a well-received biographical novel by Swiss writer Eveline Hasler, *Flying with Wings of Wax.* It is based on the life of Emily Kempin, born in 1853, the first woman to study law at the University of Zurich. After she earned her doctorate, she was not allowed to try cases in court, because she was not a man. The United States was the only place at the time where a woman could hope to practice and teach law. Emigration to New York was made possible by her determined pursuit of her career, but also because her husband Walter fulfilled the role of homemaker. Emily entered a circle of high-society feminists, and with their support started a law school for women that was eventually adopted by New York University. After her success in America, Emily returned to Zurich, where her life and her strength crumbled under professional frustration, a growing rift between her and her husband, and the marriage of the man with whom she had fallen in love to her 19-year-old daughter. Emily spent her last few years institutionalized, well looked after as befitted wealthy society, and all but forgotten (Hasler 1994).

CONCLUSION

The basic agreement between culture and social structure in Switzerland is in the importance of the middle categories. The strength of the middle class goes hand in hand with a national character that dislikes extremes on most value dimensions. Pragmatism and consensus prevail over grandeur and radical innovation. The state is active in cultural policy as well as in those that express society's responsibility for the welfare of the individual, thereby reinforcing consolidation toward the middle ground, at least in intent. This activism has favored, rather than diminished, the wealth of local cultures and communities. Most notably, the coexistence of four language communities is appreciated. This is possible also because the language communities are separated in space, and thus the demands that multilingualism makes on the individuals are small.

If culture and social structure make for stability in many aspects of Swiss life, there are unstable elements as well. Because of the country's small size, and of the minority position that each language community holds among people of the same language in neighboring countries, the national identity of the Swiss has remained volatile, sometimes to the extent of denying their existence. Recent developments in both culture and social structure have heightened their identity problems. The media revolution turns people increasingly toward foreign sources of meaning and inspiration. The economy has so changed under the onslaught of **globalization** that social inequality has increased despite the egalitarian culture and a successful welfare state. That the Swiss have not yet woken up to massive social disparities may be due largely to the positions of foreigners and women who fill the lower ranks. The interaction of culture and social structure is particularly graphic in the occupational structure, education, and family roles of these two groups.

Change has accelerated. This is producing new cultural dimensions as well as new phenomena of social mobility. The social and cultural distance between those who look back nostalgically and those embracing modernity has become larger. English may be on the way to becoming a fifth national language. The Swiss have begun to experience downward mobility in significant numbers. Many more young have to change occupations during their lifetime than was usual for their parents. But we have also seen that the barriers to mobility are not the same everywhere. For example, education remains a more important impediment to intergenerational mobility in Switzerland than in the United States, whereas business ownership is less important.

The balance between the forces of constancy and those of change has thus been altered. Many local elements favor constancy, but they are put on the defensive by the changes that cross the borders of this small country almost unhindered. The stability that Switzerland inherited from its special position in the history of the first half of the century is waning.

Basic Institutions

In the seventies when I was studying in Germany, an official from the Cantonal Department of Education in my Swiss hometown contacted me. Would I be so kind as to pick up a scholarship for which I qualified? I had not known my rights and complied happily. Some years earlier, I had attended the Gymnasium *there, a distant equivalent of high school, as the only working-class child in my class. My parents worried I might not be "socially fit," and it took some special convincing by my primary school teacher to let me sit for the entrance exam. I do remember periods of awkwardness because I never dressed fashionably and did not feel good enough to go with all the others to dance school, but the fact that I made it through university had more to do with financial aid readily provided by government and private sources and less with white handkerchiefs and chances to find dates at the "Higher Daughters' School" across the* Gymnasium *park. Obviously, the barriers regulating access to education were different from what Americans would expect, and they still are.*

This chapter deals with institutions that are commonly thought to instill the basic values of society as well as many of the techniques to get around in it: religion, education, and family. In many respects, their Swiss versions are not significantly different from those of surrounding countries. For example, it is hard to distinguish family patterns in Switzerland and Germany by more than matters of degree. Compared to the United States, however, some of the differences seem more important. Some are historical; for example, church and state in Switzerland have never been separated completely. Others have more to do with the way modern society views the place of the institutions within the total fabric. Until recently, the Swiss treated education as a passage in life that ends with adolescence and that for each individual leads through one of several exclusive tracks. Opinions about the health and future development of families are widely divided, but families in Switzerland have not become sufficiently dysfunctional to inspire a generalized values malaise. By and large, the Swiss see their primary agents of socialization as less problematic than the economy, the environment, or even their political system.

RELIGION: STRONG HERITAGE, SECULARIZED SOCIETY

Church Taxes Collected by the State

There is little in the present-day religious situation of Switzerland that is particularly Swiss. Both in spirituality and in the organized aspects of religion, the similarities with other central European countries are more important than the differences. They are even more striking with Germany, a country that started the Reformation movement in the 16th century. In both countries, the religious map is dominated by two denominations of nearly equal weight. The state recognizes the Catholic Church as well as the one national Protestant church and relies on their contribution for social service programs. Also the state collects church taxes on their behalf. These arrangements are time-honored; they sanctioned the end to religious strife and the difficult coexistence that kept the Catholic and Protestant communities socially separate until the early 20th century. These divisions had often been territorial, so that in Switzerland some of the cantons, sovereign small states until 1848, decided to be purely Catholic and others Protestant. More recent times have seen the religious factor grow continuously weaker in public life. This section will therefore be limited to reporting the Swiss position on some common religious trendlines. It will show that the autonomy of the individual has been firmly established in Swiss religious life.

In the 1990 census, 40 percent of the population reported themselves as Protestants. Catholics accounted for 46 percent. The remaining 14 percent belonged to other religious communities or said they were nonbelievers. Among the non-Christian faiths, Moslems, almost exclusively from among foreign workers, are by far the most important: about 2 percent of the population profess Islam.

The social structure of Protestants and Catholics has in many respects become very similar. The Protestants have largely lost their historic lead in education, urbanity, and higher occupations. There is still a territorial association, with some rural cantons having remained largely Catholic. In the historically Protestant cantons, which were industrialized earlier, the mixing of populations has gone very far. Geneva, once considered the world capital of Protestantism, now has a Catholic community double the size of the Protestants, due to domestic mobility as well as immigration. Only the federal capital, Berne, is surrounded by a canton with a clear Protestant majority to this day. Religious boundaries in everyday interaction outside church events have completely broken down; in 1989, 37 percent of all new marriages were **interdenominational.** Many people do not even know the religious affiliations of friends and close neighbors.

Religious Diversity Grows Slowly, in Urban Centers

The important point to make is that in Switzerland, religious and language boundaries do not coincide. The two largest language regions, German and French, both contain a number of historically Catholic and Protestant cantons. To an extent, religious and language group interests neutralize each other; this is in part why sectional conflict has remained weak. One of the major political parties does have a power base in the traditional Catholic cantons, but even it has found it expedient to revise its appeal for a broader audience.

A correlation of some interest is the one between religious communities and the urban–rural dimension. Catholics are, relative to the other religious communities and the nonaffiliated, the ones with the strongest roots in the countryside. Nontraditional Christians and other religious groups have grown primarily in the shelter that urban environments offered them from the pressures of social conformity. This growth is recent, chiefly after 1970. In 1960, only 2 percent of the resident population did not belong to either mainstream church. Thirty years later, this figure stands at 14 percent. Most of the growth is from immigration rather than conversion of residents. It demonstrates the accelerated cultural diversity of the country, spearheaded by the cities.

In addition to the greater diversity of religious affiliations (and lack of religion), the internal state of the major denominations has been significantly modified in recent decades. The change concerns both the belief systems and the place of the churches in society. Protestants and Catholics have become less attached to biblical doctrines. Members recognize the authority of the churches selectively, by personal decision.

Churches Are Christian, but Beliefs Are Broadly Humanistic

Melich (1991: 181–242) surveyed religious attitudes as part of her study of Swiss values in 1989. According to her, a strong majority of the Swiss believe in the existence of God (87 percent). The belief in a divine spirit, a higher power, or a life force is popular (64 percent), whereas the traditional concept of a personal God is held by only 24 percent of the people. This distinguishes Catholics (33 percent hold onto God as a person) clearly from Protestants (16 percent). A bit illogically, a higher percentage look forward to their own resurrection as individual persons (48 percent). The devil is not in good books with the Swiss; only 28 percent are ready to personify the spiritual force of evil (Melich 1991: 209). These results are confirmed by a study that used a different typology (reported in Kreis 1993: 226). It classified 51 percent of the interviewees as "religious

TABLE 9

Authority of the Churches in Personal
and Social Ethical Questions

Issue	Percentage Who Recognize the Churches' Authority
Racial discrimination	57%
Third-World debt	49
Euthanasia	48
Arms race	43
Abortion	40
Unemployment	34
Pre- and extramarital sex	33
Homosexuality	30

Source: Anna Melich, ed., *Les valeurs des Suisses* (Berne: Peter Lang S.A., 1991), p. 220.

humanists," that is, believing in God, but not specifically Christian; 25 percent as Christians with a broadminded spirituality; and 7 percent as exclusivist Christians.

The distance taken from classical Christian doctrines is considerable. Not surprisingly, then, the people who recognize the authority of the churches in personal and ethical questions are also in a minority. Melich (1991: 220) presented a number of issues and asked her study subjects about the moral competence of the churches. This authority was more readily conceded for issues that need wide-ranging policies (I have marked them with italics in Table 9) than for those that call for personal decisions.

The difference is slight but significant: Despite religious individualization, the Swiss expect the churches to accomplish collective tasks, notably in social services. Approval rates for such involvements are high: 90 percent agree that the churches should offer organized care for the elderly; 65 percent want them to cooperate in Third-World projects (Kreis 1993: 229). Of all the programs, public and private, for the rehabilitation of drug addicts, the one run by a politically clever pastor in Zurich is probably the best known in the country. The widely recognized presence of the churches in social programs and the distance that a majority of citizens keep in matters of faith balance out: On a scale of the overall confidence that various institutions in Switzerland enjoy, the churches take a middle position, worse than all kinds of government authorities (who, as we have seen, enjoy high overall trust), but better than the banks, international organizations, big corporations, the unions, and the media (Melich 1991: 52).

Between self-declared spirituality and confidence in the institutional churches on the one hand and actual participation in church activities on the other, there is a wide gap. Church attendance is low, perhaps similar to that in surrounding countries, but considerably lower than in

TABLE 10

Church Attendance of Protestants and Catholics
in a Typical Week

	Switzerland, 1989	United States, 1987
Protestant	17%	38%
Catholic	39	53
National	**29**	**40**

Sources: Anna Melich, ed., *Les valeurs des Suisses* (Berne: Peter Lang S. A., 1991), p. 200; and Richard T. Schaefer and Robert P. Lamm, *Sociology* (New York: McGraw-Hill, 1989), p. 370.

the United States. This can be safely assumed at least for the Protestants. After some extrapolation of Melich's data (1991: 200) to make measures somewhat comparable, Table 10 can be created.

Besides attendance of liturgical events, activism in religious organizations is also a sign of the churches' vitality. In Melich's sample, 11 percent said they were active beyond general church membership. In the life of Swiss voluntary associations, the churches rank behind sports clubs (23 percent) and professional organizations (13 percent) but ahead of the protection of nature (10 percent), charities (9 percent), and political parties (9 percent) (35 percent of the Swiss do not belong to any voluntary association Melich 1991: 150). Organized religious activism is therefore clearly a minority affair. But this is not to be confounded with the extent of tithing: many nominal members who rarely or never go to church pay church tax as a *voluntary* part of their tax bill.

The major churches have had to respond to the individualization of society, the declining authority of doctrine, and the offers from new faith communities and lifestyles. "A la carte" religious activities try to honor a need for choice and let everybody in the parish find something of his or her taste (Kreis 1993: 302). Discrete borrowings from New Age currents enrich traditional liturgy. In the church where in the days of my youth you could hear a needle fall, the baptisms in a recent service were accompanied with ritual dancing. After the formal service, a barbecue and potluck lunch was shared in the rear pew area near the entrance, enlarged with red and white wines, and uplifted to the tunes of a folklore duo. To an outsider, the styles used in the event did not always harmonize, but many of the parish members obviously liked to express their faith through their bodies and appetites within the church walls, both inconceivable 30 years ago.

No Strong "Christian Right"

The dominance of just two denominations, both of them in long-standing cooperation with the state, has also immunized Switzerland against major political movements rising from religious quarters. There is nothing like the strong "Christian right" in the United States. The reasons are many. Church members who wish to express their convictions on political platforms are likely drawn to the existing Christian Democratic Party and (the less important) Protestant Popular Party, who are players of the political center. The idea that Switzerland was God's chosen country enjoyed brief popularity in the 18th century but was later replaced by secular conceptions of the democratic nation. Modern patriotism rests on language, folklore, and history; it uses religious references rarely in anthems, in the opening invocation of the Constitution, and in official oaths. The clergy, most of whom were trained in the theological departments of state universities, tend to have somewhat left-of-the-center views. Paid by their parish council with tax monies, they do not have to please the local tastes of a check-writing audience. They are social service managers just as much as they are evangelists and function in dense organizational networks with schools, adult education, welfare, and social security services. School prayer, abortion, and homosexuality are rarely discussed. Prayers contain references to the environment, the Third World, or new poverty, all in civil tones. One often has the feeling that church language maintains just enough distinction from the ambient society in order to justify a continued institutional existence, but not to alienate supporters.

Is all that of consequence for the position of religion in Swiss society? By many indicators, Switzerland has become as highly a secularized country as other rich nations except the United States. Traditional beliefs have faded, institutional participation has declined, and moral questions have assumed a nonreligious character. New religious ideas, once Switzerland's strong contribution to the Reformation had ended, have come from abroad. In this century, they have not yet made any major impact on Swiss society. Short of radical change elsewhere in Europe, there is little reason to believe that the religious factor will grow stronger.

EDUCATION: IT'S FOR ALL YOUR LIFE, SON!

Twenty-six Educational Systems

We have seen that education is a particularly powerful resource for the attainment of professional status in Switzerland. The education system holds a key place not only for work and business, but for the transmission of culture at large. And like other segments of Swiss cultural life, it followed the post-war modernization processes of the Western world slowly. Higher education did not begin its significant expansion until the late sixties, and then in response to changes in the occupational structure that had already taken place (Levy et al. 1997: Ch. 4, p. 69). Between 1960 and 1995, the number of university students grew more than fourfold, but enrollment has remained lower than in other countries. For example, for every 1,000 in the population, there are 20 persons currently taking tertiary-level education.[2] Germany, which has an education system in many respects similar to that of the Swiss, has 28; the United States, with a rate of 58 out of 1,000, clearly outdistances Switzerland (Levy et al. 1997: Ch. 4, p. 8).

Despite its expansion in the last 30 years, the Swiss system has retained some of its basic characteristics. It is

> essentially the responsibility of the cantons. Thus it is not really correct to talk of a Swiss educational system, but only of several independent and differing systems. The distribution of responsibility and authority between the Confederation, the cantons and the communities, as well as collaboration with private institutions, is characteristic of Switzerland's federalist structure and has historical roots. . . [In] the cantonal school systems, following a voluntary period of kindergarten fully financed by the state, most cantons stipulate nine years' compulsory schooling (in a few cantons it is eight years). This compulsory schooling (German: *Volksschule*) for all children capable of normal education consists of a primary school period of four, five or six years. There then follows a choice of schooling which puts varying demands upon the pupils and is known collectively as secondary level I. Attendance is free of charge. The *Volksschule* usually pass their pupils on to either vocational training or into secondary level II. Vocational training is based on a dual system consisting of practical training with a company and parallel attendance at least once a week at a vocational school which provides instruction in general subjects. Secondary level II consists of high schools (*Maturitätsschulen*) and diploma schools. The high schools provide intellectually gifted children with a broad general education and prepare them for university. The diploma schools, a mixture between the vocational schools and the high schools, prepare the pupils over a period of two to three years for vocational training at a non-university tertiary college. [CCPSA 1993b: 1]

Tracks Difficult to Change

The succinct summary does not necessarily bring out the full importance of the dual system. In the United States, the majority of young people complete their educational careers with a general high school degree, and "large segments of the American population. . . are therefore virtually indistinguishable in terms of education" (Charles and Buchmann 1994: 615). For the majority of young Swiss, the end of formal education occurs with their acquisition of an occupation-specific credential. More than 70 percent enter vocational training after compulsory schooling. This is mostly in the form of an apprenticeship between the ages of 16 and 19. The apprenticeship is regulated by a contract between the employer and the apprentice. Craft and trade associations play an important part in establishing job descriptions, training programs, and examination rules. There are about 270 different, federally recognized trades (the German word is *Beruf*, which is semantically

---

2. Tertiary education, roughly, is college-level education, but is usually started at age 20, after 13 or 14 years of primary and secondary schooling.

The self-image: "Paese del burro," Italian for "Land of butter." In a freeway rest stop area, a billboard projects a rural idyll. Photographer, Matthias Wehrlin.

close to vocation, traditionally implying a lifelong endeavor). The basic focus of the apprenticeship is practical, which guarantees that the trainees are already highly productive before graduation. They earn wages during that period. But it also means that three-quarters of the young Swiss do not meet university prerequisites through their normal education, and later on find it hard to change tracks. The system is impervious in two ways: Barriers between vocational and academic tracks are high (they are being lowered), and the need for recurrent and lifelong education is only gradually asserting itself. Rather, the education certificates are taken as a fixed-size resource at the end of adolescence to be used through the rest of life. This, too, is changing slowly. Still, the idea of a "second chance" in education is not at the heart of Swiss culture.

Teachers Are Expensive, but Education Remains Affordable

Some of the inequality that educational typing creates is corrected by the universally high quality of the education. Teachers in all branches are well paid and work in well-equipped schools. Primary school teacher entry-level salaries vary between $45,000 and $60,000 annually. A high school teacher, toward the end of his career, may make as much as $125,000. Teachers and vocational instructors are, therefore, well motivated. Special education is offered for many of the foreign children who come from other cultural backgrounds. Some parents are concerned about schools with a high percentage of foreign children, but there is no inner-city school syndrome, and so far little violence in schools. The quality differences between universities are also smaller than in the United States, and fees are modest. A student at Zurich University pays about $1,100 per year, regardless of the number of courses taken. The state offers poor students scholarships that also take care of some of the living costs. Inequality is further mitigated by the importance and easier accessibility of nonuniversity tertiary-education institutions. While only 8 percent of the population between 25 and 64 years of age have a university degree in Switzerland (United States: 24 percent), 13 percent have diplomas from higher technical and vocational schools (United States: 7 percent).

Strong Social Barriers

The barriers that keep many young Swiss out of university education are less of a financial than of a social and cultural nature. Gender, region, and parental education are still strong discriminating factors. I spoke of the gender factor in the section on women. Regional disparities are patent: Of the 19-years-of-age cohort in 1993, 16 percent had *Maturität* certificates opening university for them. In the urban, historically Protestant, French-speaking canton of Geneva, that figure was up to 32 percent. Conversely, in rural, Catholic, German-speaking Appenzell-Innerrhoden, a mere 8 percent qualified (Federal Office of Statistics 1995a: 111). The ratio between those extremes is roughly 4:1. Social barriers are even higher. That expanded education "has hardly led to openings for the less privileged sections of the population" is not the view of some radicals, but an official government position (CCPSA, 1993c: 2). Chances to attend university are 13 times greater for those of academic parents than for those whose parents completed mandatory *Volksschule* only (Federal Office of Statistics, 1996a: 5).

The expansion of higher education and the persistence of social barriers to access have changed the influence of the education system on social inequality. The growing number of university graduates has lowered the value of certificates in the job market. The relationship between level of education and occupational status is somewhat looser than it was a few years ago. The same amount of education "buys" less status in measurable terms: Levy and others have shown that respondents who shared the education level of their parents had a two and a half times greater likelihood to sink than to rise vis-à-vis the parental socioprofessional standing (Levy et al. 1997: Ch. 6, p. 10). This is particularly discomforting for those in the lower classes who are still finding access to higher education very difficult. Its spectacular growth over the past three decades has certainly benefited the middle class, has not harmed the upper class, and may not have helped the lower class as much as expected. As Switzerland tries to pull up to international levels of enrollment in higher education, expansion will only further marginalize the lower class unless some of these barriers can be lowered further.

FAMILIES: MORE SINGLES, BUT NO VALUES CRISIS
Greater Tolerance for
Nontraditional Arrangements

As late as 1990, Swiss sociologists could write that in the areas of marriage and divorce, "Switzerland is not fundamentally different from other countries, although the Swiss marry a bit more and divorce a bit less" (Kellerhals and Coenen-Huther 1990: 121). Already a few years later, when the first analyses of the 1990 census were published, at least the part about divorce had to be revised. Yet their point remains valid to a large extent. In their basic social functions, Swiss families do not fundamentally differ from those of other advanced Western nations. For example, small **nuclear families** predominate; three-generation families have become just about as rare as elsewhere. In comparing with other societies, there are many matters of degree, and no sharp breaks. As we shall see, Swiss families are solid midfield in some aspects and laggards in others. They are not front-runners.

The Swiss family landscape is difficult to paint on a single flat panel. Since World War II, society has become more tolerant of varied private arrangements (Fleiner-Gerster and Lüscher 1991: 513), with the result that a diversity of family forms developed. These have become a recognized plurality because the media cover them extensively. Due to the media's need for simplification, highly contrasted views of the Swiss family's recent evolution are held. One side sees traditionalism defend itself successfully. This is documented by the fact that 60 percent of the population live in families with children and that 72 percent of all privately housed persons are members of a household with a married couple, with or without children (Federal Office of Statistics 1994a: 8). The opposite view stresses the individualization of society. Single-person households have become a very important group (32 percent in 1990), and couples without other family members account for more than a quarter of all households (27 percent) (Federal Office of Statistics 1994b: 48–51).

The contrast is largely spurious. It may have more to do with the ways journalists read census tables than with sharp distinctions in reality. This becomes obvious when we realize that the singles and couples without other family members (59 percent of all households) make up only 35 percent of the population. More revealing than static oppositions is a dynamic view over time (see Table 11).

Single-person households as an alternative to traditional forms of family life have indeed markedly grown over the past three decades. Their growth was particularly strong between 1970 and 1980 when the cultural revolution took root in private lifestyles. During the entire three decades, however, one-person households in Switzerland were less predominant than in the United States, and in the eighties their relative growth was slower.

TABLE 11

Growth of Single-Person Households

Year	Switzerland	United States
1960	14.2%	21.5%
1970	19.7	N/A
1980	29.0	32.3
1990	32.4	37.1

Note: As a percentage of all households. US value for 1990 projected.

Sources: Switzerland: Federal Office of Statistics, *The 1990 Population Census: Switzerland in Profile* (Berne: Federal Office of Statistics, 1994), p. 51; United States: Richard T. Schaefer and Robert P. Lamm, *Sociology* (New York: McGraw-Hill, 1989), p. 321.

But "Single" Does Not Always Mean "Self-Determined"

A number of factors are thought to have caused this evolution. Growing life expectancy, particularly for women, leads to more frequent singles' episodes in old age. The young are getting married later. Also they married slightly less frequently in 1990 than in 1960 (the marriage rate fluctuates a lot). But above all, the Swiss divorce much more often. Since the sixties, the divorce rate has tripled. We shall return to this in a moment.

Singles live more in cities, families more in the countryside, but urbanization has not only increased free choices. Particularly among the elderly, many continue to live alone in cities for lack of more attractive arrangements elsewhere. Lüscher and Thierbach (1994: 38) have warned against celebrating signs of modernity wherever we find large concentrations of single-person households. For example, they found that the risk to be single was 226 percent higher for workers in the textile and leather industry than for the population at large. This group includes a high number of single women over age 60 who are too poor to retire and therefore go on working in this declining sector of the economy. Conversely, when we find the media workers to have a 146 percent higher likelihood to live single, we are more inclined to assume self-elected life styles in a modern, expanding sector of the economy. Total household figures combine very different partial changes in society, and the term *individualization* can have several meanings.

Divorce Has Tripled, but Not to American Levels

Public debate on the situation of families in the United States is often alarmist about the breakdown of family values. The Swiss have developed a more pragmatic understanding of family and marriage. The nuclear family continues to exert normative guidance and actually is what

TABLE 12

Divorce Rates in Selected Countries

Country	Divorce Rate
Sweden	50%
United States	48
Switzerland	37
Germany	30
Italy	7

Sources: United States (1987): Richard T. Schaefer and Robert P. Lamm, *Sociology* (New York: McGraw-Hill, 1989), p. 338; other countries: Federal Office of Statistics, *Statistisches* Jahrbuch der Schweiz 1996. Separatdruck Kapital 1: Bevölkerng (Zurich: Verlog Neve Zürcher Zeitung, 1996).

the majority practices. But much of that is due to immigration—foreign workers were reunified with their family members when immigration law became more mellow on family unification—as well as to generational effects. A strong Swiss baby-boomer generation started families, evident in resurgent marriage rates from 1976 to 1991 (in that, Switzerland differed from all surrounding countries, whose people became less inclined to marry during the eighties). In this generation, many consider their first marriage a trial run. Others live as consensual couples for some years; for them marriage is closely tied to the arrival of the first child. Family law is cautiously adapting to the results of social change. Still its current revision places the institutional character of marriage above contractual aspects. But Swiss society by and large recognizes the individual's sovereignty in choosing forms of living together. In most milieux, divorce is no longer a moral issue, although its actual frequency varies by a factor of 1 to 4 between the rural Catholic cantons and the urban areas of Protestant extraction. Most religious groups also consider divorce a necessary and wholesome adaptation of the family institution to modern life. When we compare its occurrence across countries (see Table 12), Switzerland, together with the other Germanic countries and with France, holds a middle position in Europe; it is some 10 percentage points lower than the US rate.

The reasons for the growing divorce rate in Switzerland are multiple, and they are in no recognizable ways different from those that operate in other countries. The expansion of female employment has reduced the relative cost for women to leave marriage; 70 percent of the divorces are nowadays initiated by women. With increasing practice, a self-reinforcing process has set in because the social stigma has lessened, and it is easier to find a new partner from the pool of other divorcees. As a more recent phenomenon, the economic recession of the nineties is motivating a growing number of divorces because couples can no longer invest in marriage-specific goods, such as family homes, that easily.

TABLE 13

Variations from Traditional Family Behavior

Country	Births to Unmarried Mothers	Teenage Fertility	One-Parent Households with Dependent Children
Sweden	47%	13	18%
United States	30	64	25
Germany	16	13	9
Switzerland	6	5	13
Italy	6	9	5

Indicators and sources: Births to unmarried mothers; as percent of all births (1992): eurostat, ed., *Begegnung in Zahlen. Ein statistisches Porträt der Schweiz im Europäischen Wirtschaftsraum* (Luxembourg: Amt für amtliche Veröffentlichungen der Europäischen Gemeinschaft, 1992), p. 6. Teenage fertility, number of births per 1,000 women aged 15–19 (1990–1995): M. Kearl, "Kearl's Guide to the Sociology of the Family," http://www.Trinity.edu/~mkearl, Trinity University, 1996. One-parent households with dependent children, as percent of total households with children (1991): "The Family. Home Sweet Home," *The Economist*, September 9, 1995, p. 26. Switzerland's value for one-parent households is for 1990.

Out-of-Wedlock Births Are Much Rarer Than in the United States

If the divorce rate increased steeply in both the United States and Switzerland, as it did, the absence of a family-values crisis in the latter country must have different reasons. The Swiss are more alarmed over growing poverty and how this is selectively affecting some families than over a breakdown of the traditional family that has not taken place. Apart from the fact that family values are a slogan of a conservative cultural revolution (which Switzerland is not undergoing), a major difference concerns illegitimate children. Switzerland has significantly fewer births to unmarried women than even its culturally close neighbor Germany and is way down from the United States. The difference is even starker when we consider teenage pregnancy. Swiss teenagers have babies 13 times less often than their American peers. A higher proportion of teenagers grow up in two-parent households where only one parent works full-time. Since the AIDS epidemic, sex education and access to contraceptives have been expanded, giving youth greater control over their intimate lives. Table 13 presents three indicators of what would be considered family disorganization in a conservative perspective.

Births to unmarried women, because there are so few, account for only 7 percent of all one-parent households in Switzerland (46 percent of such households stem from the death of one parent, 43 percent from divorce or separation). The vulgar specter of welfare mothers breeding society and government into bankruptcy simply does not appear under these circumstances.

Low teenager fertility is one of many indicators of the social climate within existing families. The Swiss, when they do marry, settle for a relatively conservative arrangement of family roles. This is particularly true of the place reserved for women. As Bretscher-Spindler (1994: 75) has succinctly formulated: "Professional careers are available to men with or without family, but only to women without family." The obstacles that women face in employment have been discussed previously, and we only have to provide a reminder here of how crippling the lack of organized child care is for the professional development of many Swiss women. At current capacity, only one in every six children for whom care is sought finds a place. But regardless of the presence of children or not, division of work in the household is firmly constant. Time-budget studies have shown that in 1979/80, Swiss men assumed 13 percent of the household chores. By 1991, the share went up to 21 percent. It is hardly affected by children, work status, or husbands' attitudes that marriage should follow egalitarian norms. The burden on mothers of employment, household work, and child care has been eased less by shifts in marital power than by having fewer children. In 1960, 28 percent of all families with children had three or more; in 1990, this figure stood at 15 percent.

Husbands Cannot Be Reformed: Accept Them, or Leave Them

The erosion of traditional family lifestyles in Switzerland has been slow, but it is real. The reduction of the marriage rate is an accessory to it, but not a very important one. The Swiss have continued to marry with unpredictably fluctuating frequency. Alternatively, they have increasingly formed consensual couples. The conception that partners have of their family roles has become more egalitarian over time, but beyond the greater labor participation of women, that has not greatly affected practice. A booming number among those who are dissatisfied with their marriage take the divorce option. They use, in sociological terms, exit rather than voice. The return to the single status seems to be easier than the change of the inner condition of a marriage. In this sense, both positions of the public debate come true: The individualists stay in, or return to, the large group of singles; the ones who keep living in families carry on with remarkable traditionalism.

CONCLUSION

As already announced in the chapter introduction, the most striking finding is the surprisingly small degree of difference vis-à-vis other Central European societies. While Switzerland's political and economic history are markedly distinct from theirs, a strong convergence is observed for the modern-day basic institutions. This is much less true when comparing with the United States. On the whole, the Swiss seem more "relaxed" about the functioning of their basic institutions. There is no family values crisis; there are no politically vociferous religious groups; and education remains affordable and of good quality (though culturally not always accessible). The individualization of society has advanced greatly, although this is not visible in all the basic institutions alike. Relatively speaking, individual autonomy is best recognized in the religious realm; receives better respect in the family (due to the availability of consensual arrangements and divorce); and continues to encounter the strongest obstacle to personal choice in the educational field, with its strong separation of tracks. This may not be a coincidence, given the importance, particularly in Switzerland, of education for the attainment of professional status. But again, these are matters of degree. Overall, the Swiss do not think that their families, schools, and organized religious communities are oppressive, or that they are failing in their socializing tasks.

CHAPTER 4

Swiss Politics

*W*ho *is the president of Switzerland? Ask, and many citizens will not know. But they will say that the president of the* **Confederation,** *as he is known, is not that important. They will know some or all the names of the seven* **Federal Councilors,** *the members of the top executive body among whom the presidency rotates. And they will know that the parties who form the* **federal** *government have been cooperating for many decades. The institutional arrangement will mean more to them than the names.*

And rightly so. The political system of Switzerland has been extremely stable. Coalition governments formed by the same parties have succeeded each other for almost 40 years. All major political forces have been integrated in the ruling coalition. Moreover, the traditions that govern Swiss politics—frequent popular ballots on propositions and bills; intense cooperation between central government and lower, but autonomous, political units; neutrality in foreign affairs—enjoy high prestige with major sections of the citizenry.

It is, therefore, tempting to begin the analysis of the Swiss political system by the description of its most important formal **institutions.** *Such an approach would be misleading. For one thing, Swiss governance relies heavily on a symbiosis of government and voluntary organizations (Hotz 1979). Political parties and special-interest associations inform the political agenda and the decision-making process through elaborate consultation systems. They also have a strong hand in administering the outcomes. Second, some of the key institutions that the American reader may take for granted are absent in the Swiss system. For example, the highest court of law in Switzerland, the Federal Tribunal, does not have jurisdiction in constitutional matters.*

*The way to go in this chapter is to work from the environment toward the system. Swiss society is divided along several dimensions that shape political attitudes, voter behavior, and recruitment to parties and other politically active organizations; these will be delineated. History and modern practice have reinforced traditions that are deeply institutionalized; the three most important traditions—***direct democracy, neutrality,*** and ***federalism—***are presented in*

some detail. Political parties and interest associations form intermediaries be-
tween society and government institutions: Their boundaries with the latter are
particularly thin and transparent in Switzerland. Diminished by the influence
of those special-interest organizations, the formal organs of government such as
the federal cabinet and parliament carry an air of perfunctory consummation
of deals made ahead of their deliberations. But the power elite, whose members
hold multiple positions in business, trade unions, administration, and army, are
time and again challenged by **social movements.** *These loose coalitions of orga-*
nized groups and sympathizers with particular stances on burning issues use
the instruments of Swiss direct democracy to keep the elite on their toes. We de-
scribe how in the process the movements themselves become domesticated and
partly integrated with the elite through compromise and consensus. While other
small countries in Europe also use consensus politics, the Swiss variant suffers
less violence in the process.

The reader may look forward to a fairly long chapter. This treatment is
justified because, as I said in the introduction, it is in her political system that
Switzerland is most keenly distinct from other advanced Western societies. To
understand Switzerland means, in no small measure, to look into the inner
workings of her body politic.

RIFTS IN SOCIETY AND POLITICS

Major cleavages in society prefigure the political camps that we expect to
see in a country, although not in a strict one-to-one correspondence. Institutional mechanisms also intervene, and the configurations of political
life have their own inertia that sometimes has them lag behind the development of new categories and processes in the ambient society. For
Western Europe, a famous thesis—the "freezing hypothesis" by Lipset
and Rokkan (1985 [1967])—holds that the political party systems in the
sixties reflected the essential cleavages that their societies had shown at
the end of the First World War (yes, the first! 1914–18). For example, the
strength of **socialist** parties in various countries was in proportion with
the brutality of the repression that the working class had suffered in the
twenties and thirties.

Similarly, politics in the nineties in part responds to new formations that took shape in society in the decades following the Second
World War, notably the growth of a much broader and better educated
middle class. The classical political divisions—between religious denominations, language and ethnic groups, town and country, socialist **left**
and conservative **right**—are deforming like blocks of ice on a slowly
moving glacier, sometimes with sudden breaks. In Switzerland, old po-
larities maintain themselves selectively, and new cleavages have appeared. Secularization and migration have weakened the religious
dimension in Swiss politics, but not to a degree that would have wiped
out all religiously based power: Because the Catholic cantons were
largely rural, with slower industrial development than in the Protestant

and urban cantons, few non-Catholic migrants arrived to challenge the dominance of the Christian Democratic Party in those regions. The left–right dimension is no longer so closely associated with **social classes.** Many of the principal backers of the traditional left, the blue-collar workers, were replaced by immigrants, ascended to the middle class, or defected to right-wing populist parties. Language groups in Switzerland are concentrated in certain regions: The interests of language minorities have therefore been dominating politics in their cantons, obviating the need for language-based parties at the federal level. Nevertheless, since the beginnings of the nineties, the linguistic differences have become more important although no major political party has so far based its appeal on the fact. Two entirely new and barely publicized cleavages have opened in the last two decades: Winners and losers of the modernization process have started to rally on opposing political poles, and within the middle classes, managers and professionals in big organizations express distinct political values (Kriesi 1995: 138).

The political elite, in their quest for reliable majorities, have reduced the complexity of their constituency to a few dimensions. In Switzerland, the left–right dimension is still the dominant one in elite politics. But a second dimension has lately become stronger. Under the assault of fast changes in the world economy, the Swiss are more sharply divided between **traditionalists** and **cosmopolitans,** cutting across the left–right antagonism. All parties are being plagued by internal tensions between modernizers and conservatives. The former want a stronger central government for many issues; the latter are defending undiluted federalism. In large measure, this polarity so far has absorbed the country versus town, Catholic versus others, and language oppositions. But the risk of language groups expressing themselves more strongly in politics is real: The French- and Italian-speaking communities, traditionally upholders of federalism, strongly desire that Switzerland join the **European Economic Area,** a move their German-speaking compatriots, dominated by traditionalists, reject. It is therefore possible that society will add a third dimension—language—to the political arena that the elite have so far kept as a flat two-dimensional surface.

THREE TIME-TESTED TRADITIONS

Direct Democracy: More Extensive Than in the United States

Switzerland is considered the only country where public life is truly determined by institutions of direct democracy. We call a democracy direct when a substantial proportion of major political decisions are provoked and decided by the citizens' direct action. Various forms of formal citizen participation produce final political decisions in addition to, and often correcting, those taken by elected representatives. The United States also has some such institutions (Auer 1989); however, these do not operate at the federal level. California's "propositions" would be a case in point. Moreover they have a complementary function, whereas in Switzerland direct-democratic institutions have transformed the entire political fabric. As we shall see, they have exercised pressure particularly toward integrating political forces in a consensus democracy.

In Switzerland, direct democracy has developed two major instruments, one of which operates at the beginning of a decision process, and the other at the end. **Initiatives** are propositions that oblige parliaments at the concerned political tier—**communal, cantonal,** or **federal**—to prepare legislation responding to an issue and to bring it to public ballot. For example, 100,000 or more citizens can demand that the federal parliament deliberate a partial change of the Swiss Constitution and conduct a popular ballot thereupon. The initiative thus works as an initial impulsion, intended to create statutes or public measures. The second device, the **referendum** works inversely. A so-called optional referendum allows a group of concerned citizens to challenge a decision already taken by a parliament. At the federal level, 50,000 citizen signatures are required for the optional referendum. Mandatory referenda automatically have certain types of new laws and international treaties submitted to the approval of the voters. Referenda thus force popular ballots on outcomes of parliamentary politics.

The range of matters amenable to referenda and initiatives has been broadened considerably over the last 150 years. The founders of the modern federal state in 1848 would admit the direct-democratic participation only for an entirely new constitution. Later in the 19th century, the optional referendum was expanded in order to challenge new federal laws, and initiatives became admissible also for the purpose of partial changes of the federal constitution. During the economic crisis of the 1930s and perforce during World War II, government by emergency measure, often extraconstitutional, grew epidemically. In 1949, the constitution was changed so as to open Federal Emergency Acts to the referendum. Since 1977, in the context of the Cold War and of growing economic cooperation in Europe, international treaties have no longer been exempt from the scrutiny of direct democracy.

Before we document the uses that the Swiss people have made of direct democracy, it is important to note that the Swiss political elite live with the constant threat that their precariously negotiated compromises will be challenged by a referendum. The fear has given rise to a preoccupation with limiting the scope of direct-democratic instruments. Several campaigns to widen their scope were launched after World War II; most met with fierce resistance and were defeated. Notably, the right to carry new laws by popular initiative, while entrenched in all cantonal constitutions, has never been created for federal matters. Here the right of initiative is limited to constitutional changes.

Between 1848 and 1994, the federal parliament passed 1,953 bills liable to be voted in popular ballot. Of those, 192 concerned constitutional

A Swiss wedding. The army loaned the homing pigeons for the ceremony. Photographer, Matthias Wehrlin.

changes subject to mandatory referenda; the people concurred with the parliamentary decisions in 139 (72 percent) of all the questions. Of the remaining 1,761 acts of parliament amenable to optional referenda, only 122 were brought to ballot. In exactly half of those occasions, the people upheld the parliamentary acts (Kriesi 1995: 98). The total success rate for opposing acts of the federal parliament was therefore a low 6 percent.

Chances for constitutional initiatives to become the law of the land are just as slim. Between 1891 and 1994, a total of 198 federal initiatives were filed. Of these, 116 were brought to ballot (the others were withdrawn by their initiators, declared invalid, or accepted by parliament). Only 12 were accepted by the people. One of the latest success examples was the moratorium on nuclear energy adopted in 1990.

The low success rate for both referenda and initiatives leads one to think that they are not effective instruments of direct democracy. Their actual importance, however, is considerable; failures and calculated nonuse have effects that changed Swiss political life more than the rare successes did.

The referendum exerts its force by the mere threat that some capable group might take it at the end of a legislative process and thereby possibly destroy the fruit of long and difficult labors. The political elite, trying to minimize that risk, have replaced confrontation with far-reaching negotiation processes. Negotiations are pursued generally before a bill is discussed in parliament. Negotiators seek to assess and, if possible, eliminate the threat that somebody could appeal to the popular ballot. The referendum has created a culture of compromise and accommodation.

By moving the critical phases of the decision process to the **preparliamentary** arena, the referendum threat thus restricts the influence of parliament. Also it creates pressures for all major political forces to become part of the governing coalition. Yet, at the same time, it weakens the coalition. It permits political opportunism. Parties who share government responsibility can choose to make a selective case against the government by trying to fell legislation sponsored by the government or by other parties of the ruling coalition. They can also launch initiatives of which they know in advance that their coalition partners disapprove. A recent case of such behavior is presented in the box on "Direct Democracy in Action."

As for initiatives, their **manifest functions** are different from those of the referenda, but the **latent functions** of both are very similar in promoting the integration of political groups. The initiative, operating at the beginning of the decision process, obliges the political elite to devote attention and consideration to a problem. It involves the entire citizenry in constitutional and (in the cantons and communes) legislative projects. Its mobilizing function can even go further, by winning citizens who otherwise would stay distant from the political process.

At the same time, the initiatives have helped to domesticate new opposition movements. If they want to use the instrument, they have to formulate specific demands and make tactical concessions in order to broaden their support. Initiatives thereby favor moderation in opposition groups. The original far-reaching demands become difficult to pursue because the need to make allies produces splits between moderates and radicals. The opportunity costs are considerable: Campaigns focused on collecting signatures and winning the popular vote use up large amounts of movement resources. One consequence is to limit the action repertories of the movements. Another is the reinforcement of their centralizing and bureaucratic tendencies, which in turn will impose financial demands and lose some of the goodwill of the members. By all risks, opposition movements that rely on the popular initiative wind up as conventional participants in the negotiation and compromise mill of normal politics.

While rarely producing the results expected by the organizers, referendum and initiative effectively sensitize public opinion to new issues and solutions that the political elite is at first unwilling to consider. Wide debate, peaceful integration of opponents, and often decisive preparliamentary negotiations are correlates that we have already discussed. These have other unintended consequences: Direct democracy opens up the political system for influence by its environment much more radically than any other political system. In other words, the political institutions in Switzerland are less autonomous than those of different democratic constitutions.

DIRECT DEMOCRACY IN ACTION: INTERNATIONAL MIGRATION, MODERNIZATION ISSUES, DECEMBER 1, 1996

On December 1, 1996, Swiss voters were called to the ballot booths to decide on two propositions, both of which responded to issues that are bound to stay for the longer term. Moreover, the propositions exemplified the major instruments of direct democracy: **initiatives,** which invite parliament to act on a particular problem, and **referenda,** which challenge an act already passed.

The initiative in point was titled "Against Illegal Immigration." It demanded that persons entering the country illegally must not be granted the right of political asylum. Rejected asylum seekers would see their rights of appeal shortened. Employers of asylum seekers would pay wages into a government fund to defray the cost of welfare.

The initiative had been sponsored by the Swiss People's Party, the party most to the **right** of the political spectrum in the four-party government coalition. The party collected about 106,000 signatures between March 1992 and October 1993. In other words, it took 20 months to organize for it and another 37 months to bring it to the polls.

The original context had been the quadrupling of asylum seekers between 1987 and 1991. In 1991, almost 42,000 foreigners demanded asylum in Switzerland, a figure that would correspond to 1,400,000 if put in proportion with the US population. Illegal **immigration** became a number one issue in domestic politics. Since then, however, the authorities have taken measures to make asylum less attractive, and the number of the cases has dropped to roughly 17,000 per year.

The second measure concerned the labor law, which the **Federal Assembly** had modified in early 1996 in order to facilitate longer operating hours for stores and two-shift operation of businesses. The changes were intended to improve flexibility in the labor market and international competitiveness. The referendum against the law was organized by trade unions and a splinter political party as well as by some women and church groups. They protested against presumed negative consequences for female workers and the degradation of Sunday to an ordinary working day.

Remarkably, the referendum and the initiative were launched by groups who were members of, or close to, the governing coalition.

Sources: Federal Chancellery, "Volksabstimmung vom 1. Dezember 1996. Erläuterungen des Bundesrates 1996," *Neue Zürcher Zeitung,* December 2–3, 1996.

In Switzerland, shared responsibility for government and dissent with individual government policies can go hand in hand. In any event, the initiative "Against Illegal Immigration" was rejected, although narrowly (45 percent of the voters were for it). The rejection was much stronger, however, in French-speaking Switzerland; Geneva, with its international mindset, voted 70 percent no. The new labor law was decisively dismissed (67 percent no) in what analysts felt was a symbolic protest against an increasingly rough billing for the working population. Religion was a factor, too: Catholic cantons, which traditionally do not side with trade unions, joined them in this issue.

Neutrality: Old Principle Seeking Modern Interpretation

Switzerland is a neutral state in the system of European powers. It is not part of any military alliance. Notably, it is absent from the North Atlantic Treaty Organization (NATO), the defense alliance created by the United States and most western European countries after the Second World War. The Swiss **neutrality** was made permanent in 1815 when the European powers reorganized their relations after the defeat of the Napoleonic revolution.

Its roots are much older though. After the **Reformation** in the 16th century, Switzerland was a federation of small independent states (the precursors of the modern cantons) divided along the Catholic–Protestant line. Alliances with any of the foreign powers, just as intolerant in religious matters as the Swiss cantons, would have incurred violent opposition from the opposite denomination. In that situation, only passivism in foreign politics was able to avoid conflict at home and to respect the autonomy of each member state. Concurrently, the power equilibrium in continental Europe was propitious to a neutral Switzerland. In turn, the Swiss guarantee that they would stay out of armed conflict reinforced the European balance of power.

Despite its long international recognition, Swiss neutrality has never denied its instrumental character. It is a means to maintain political independence, not an ethical good in itself. Switzerland has felt free to keep trading links with countries involved in war while at the same time offering its good services as a mediator. In practice, Swiss neutrality was circumscribed by the forces of political polarization pulling on this small country. It could not avoid participating in the economic blockade against

Germany and Austria in the First World War; it made questionable economic deals with the fascist powers in the Second World War; and more recently it joined sanctions against Libya and the former Yugoslavia.

Concerned for a positive contribution to international stability and solidarity, Switzerland has been active in areas of foreign policy consonant with political and military neutrality. It has built a tradition of support for international organizations and humanitarian movements. After the First World War, it helped to found the League of Nations, the precursor organization to the United Nations. A significant contribution to the budget of the International Committee of the Red Cross, for its worldwide action for war victims, has been steadily underwritten by the federal government. But the support for international organizations is not unqualified. Although Switzerland participates in numerous United Nations agencies and hosts the administrative centers of many international organizations in Geneva, it is one of the very few nations not to be a member of the United Nations. An attempt to join was rejected by the Swiss people in 1986. A majority of the voters were concerned with the implications that United Nations membership would have for Switzerland's neutrality. The decision did not prevent the country from joining, in 1992, other international institutions such as the World Bank. Within the Organization for Security and Cooperation in Europe (OSCE), Switzerland is an active member. More immediate repercussions, however, are felt from the refusal, in an extremely contested ballot in 1992, to join the European Economic Area created by the European Union. Political neutrality, however, was but one argument used in the debate; more decisive were fears of uncontrolled immigration, interference with Swiss federalism and direct democracy, and the breakdown of the barriers that protected the domestically oriented sectors of the economy.

Different ideas about neutrality have thus also become part of the traditionalist–cosmopolitan cleavage. The larger part of the political elite and many internationally connected citizens have come to understand that in contemporary world affairs, a small country cannot take advantage of its neutrality alone and that it needs to exercise its international goodwill by participating in multilateral organizations.

So far the instruments of direct democracy have been adapted to give greater legitimacy to Switzerland's growing political connections with the world. When the authorities consider long-term international treaties or the adherence to international security organizations and supranational communities, such moves are mandatorily submitted to popular ballot. But large groups of the Swiss population are unaware of the extent of Switzerland's involvement in the wider world and hardly appreciate the opportunities that international organizations provide for solidarity and commerce. Without a deep learning process in the entire citizenry, a few formal adjustments in the toolbox of direct democracy will not buy the legitimacy for a new, courageous interpretation of Swiss neutrality.

Federalism: The Comfortable Accommodation of the Small

We have seen that the traditions of neutrality and direct democracy have deep historical roots. The revolutionary year 1848 not only wrote the powers of direct democracy into the Constitution, it also redefined the relationship between cantons and the federal government. The liberal cantons had defeated the conservative Catholic cantons; the short and mild civil war favored political compromise. The transfer of sovereignty from the cantons to the Confederation, demanded by the winners, was facilitated by an arrangement that gave small and large cantons equal standing in national politics. A two-chamber parliamentary system was created, loosely patterned on the American model, but—and this is different from the United States—with the two chambers having identical competencies. This has given, as we shall see further below, the small cantons de facto veto powers.

The modern Swiss state, therefore, was a weak state from its inception. Not only did direct democracy make it less autonomous from the interference of the ambient society; also among the tiers of government, the Confederation and the cantons deal with each other as equal partners. Philosophically, the weakness of the state has been dressed in the clothes of the "subsidiarity principle." This has a double meaning. First, problems that affect society are to be addressed by the state only when the private sector cannot solve them. Second, government activities are to be entrusted to the lowest tier possible, ideally the communes. Accordingly, the consequences of modernization in Switzerland were dealt with primarily by private organizations. An example that we have met earlier is the vocational education system. It was developed in great measure by small business associations. Private initiative did relieve the state of part of the administrative burdens, but due to the growing complexity of the tasks that private organizations discharged, over time most of them wound up depending on more and more intricate government support systems.

Within an expanding state, federal powers also grew. But their growth has remained inhibited by the constitutional principle that all powers that are not explicitly given to the Confederation remain with the cantons. It has wound its way through a considerable number of constitutional changes. Between 1874 and 1987 the federal constitution underwent 130 modifications and additions. Another 116 initiatives to change it foundered, many over resistance from alliances formed for the defense of cantonal rights.

The most massive expansion of federal competencies took place only after the Second World War. Decades of sustained and strong economic growth bolstered government finances, allowing a comprehensive social security system to be created. This era of prosperity created momentum to expand state activity on a wide range of problems that economic and social changes were creating. Environmental protection, strengthening of the position of renters and consumers, infrastructure, and land zoning were but a few areas in which private initiative had reached its limits, and for which constitutional bases and machinery were created for effective government intervention.

Despite occasional criticism of bureaucracy, it is hard to argue that the expansion of government competencies was self-induced. Public policy in Switzerland is too notoriously dictated by powerful special-interest associations. I turn to this later. If the expansion of the public sector has been contained, this is more due to stiffer economic and **fiscal** climates. This has not ruled out new adaptations of the subsidiarity principle. In some new problem areas, the state has been innovating in its relationship with the private sector. Thus, without waiting for private initiatives to come forward, public administrations have urged the private sector, with the promise of financial and other support, to set up new organizations for problem areas like alcoholism and AIDS prevention (Bütschi and Cattacin 1994).

CANTONS AND COMMUNES: BUILDING BLOCKS AND IMPLEMENTING MACHINES

A Federal Government without Field Agencies

The Swiss cantons grew out of the independent small states that together formed old Switzerland. Despite the transfer of their sovereignty to the Confederation, they have remained important political and administrative units. They elect their authorities free from federal interference. This sets Switzerland apart from other, more centralist European states. As we have already said, the cantons are not in a hierarchical relationship with the Confederation, but are partners of equal rights. The federal constitution guarantees their existence and boundaries, which, therefore, cannot be abolished or reorganized by administrative fiat.

What makes cantons doubly precious is the fact that they also provide the machinery for the implementation of most federal laws. Switzerland has few federal agencies with an administrative presence on the ground. In the American system, central government can count on its own field agencies to make it independent, in matters of implementing federal policy, of the administrative capacity of the states and counties. In Switzerland, it is the synergy between Confederation and cantons, also called *cooperative federalism*, that translates law into action. For example, federal income taxes are collected by the communes within the cantons; the Confederation does not have Internal Revenue Service field offices.

This is not a homogeneous system. In fact, we are dealing with 26 analogous and autonomous subsystems. The cantons are of very different size and economic stature (see Table 14 for the extremes). Plus, each treasures a different political tradition and constitution. The differences can take on grotesque dimensions, as exemplified by the history of voter enfranchisement. Thus, in the Canton of Neuchâtel, aliens have had the

TABLE 14

Size Variation among Swiss Cantons:
Most and Least Populous Cantons (1993)

Canton	Population	Economic Activity (US$ billions)	Tax Receipts (US$ billions)
Zurich	1,165,000	56.8	5.88
Appenzell-Inner Rhodes	15,000	.4	.05

Note: US$1 = CHF 1.20.

Source: Calculated after Hanspeter Kreisi, *Le Système Politique Suisse* (Paris: Ed. Economica, 1995), p. 71.

right to vote in cantonal matters since 1850; women (Swiss women, yes!), however, were admitted to the ballot only in 1959. In other parts of Switzerland, women were excluded from the ballot until 1990, and aliens were never invited to the polling stations. Cantonal autonomy also means that the cantons and communes have preserved the right to fix certain tax rates. This is very different from the German system, where the distribution of tax revenue among the tiers of their federal system is controlled by the highest level, the Federation.

Exchanges between Confederation and cantons are rich and diverse. They involve legal norms and budgetary support, as well as organizational resources. After all that has been said about equal partnership, we are not surprised to find two-way transactions in all those areas. Thus, the cantons have the right to initiate bills in the federal parliament. The Confederation, in turn, involves the cantons in extensive consultative procedures in legislation. The Confederation makes wide use also of expert commissions and ministerial conferences to which the cantons send their representatives. Differently from the **European Union,** the Swiss federal legislation is not bound by unanimous consent of all member states. A majority of members in both houses of parliament suffices to pass a law. But the majority principle is compromised by the very unequal size of the cantons. This allows alliances of the smaller (generally more rural and conservative) cantons to block initiatives that a large part of the Swiss people would like to advance. In the extreme, small cantons, representing as little as 20 percent of the total population, may cause, through a majority of objecting state votes, a law passed by parliament or a popular initiative to fall.

The division of labor between Confederation, cantons, and communes can be expressed also in financial terms. The Confederation contributes substantially to the cost of services rendered through the "cooperative federalism" arrangements. In total, the financial transfers to cantons and communes account for a quarter of the federal budget (see Table 15).

Taking the transfers into account, the three tiers have financial lead roles in different areas. The Confederation dominates foreign relations,

Swiss Politics

TABLE 15

Financial Transfers between Tiers

Tier	Tax receipts	Outlays after Transfers	Employees
Confederation	44%	26%	28%
Cantons	32	42	38
Communes	24	32	34
Total	100	100	100

Source: Hanspeter Kriesi, *Le Système Politique Suisse* (Paris: Ed. Economica, 1995), p. 59.

defense, agriculture, and social security. The cantons pay a large part of the bill in justice administration, public health, police and fire services, education, and research. The communes are the most active in environmental protection, cultural activities, and sports promotion. Other sectors of activity such as roads, housing, and civil protection are shared more equally.

The centralization at the federal level is, therefore, not very advanced. In fact, a tendency towards decentralization increased after World War II, with a series of new government activities created and devolved upon regional and communal tiers. What is important here is the strong position of the middle tier, the cantons. This is different from other small countries in Europe. The Netherlands, for example, spends only 2.5 percent of government budgets at this level, as against 42 percent in Switzerland (Kriesi 1995: 60). The importance of financial transfers down the tiers of the Swiss cooperative federalism has certainly contributed to the emergence of the traditionalist–cosmopolitan dimension in Swiss politics. While many observers attribute the lack of openness toward greater Europe and the world chiefly to private business, resistance comes also from the vested interests that fiscal redistribution has created and nourished in cantonal and communal administrations.

Not Only Advantages

Most Swiss will not hesitate, however, to enumerate the advantages of federalism that, for them, are obvious. This form of government provides a decision-making structure that works simultaneously at several levels. It combines long-term planning with pragmatic, local orientations. Decentralized political authority also protects those types of minorities that are concentrated in certain areas. For that reason, minority protection has worked particularly well for the language and religious communities. Nobody would ever think of making German the language of instruction in schools everywhere or to suppress school prayer in the Catholic cantons. Federalism thus responds to the cultural diversity of Switzerland. It directs discontent away from the national polity and thereby increases national cohesion. It reduces the social distance between citizens and the centers of power. It gives small political parties the chance to attain office at the communal and cantonal governments and thus trains them in the use of power before they make an entry into the national arena. Finally, the more progressive-minded collectivities are free to shelter havens of social experiments, not immediately sanctioned, and possibly later copied, by the mainstream.

Serious discussions of the drawbacks are much rarer. For one thing, the Swiss, although being democratic, do not like to discuss power. But federalism is about power. It keeps political power diffused at a time when economic power is being concentrated, both in the country and in supranational actors. The Swiss government, held back by the weight of federalist arrangements and traditions, is impotent as a discussion partner in the international fora that address economic policy.

This impotency translates into domestic affairs. The consultative mechanisms of federalism set a slow pace of decision making that makes it difficult for the Swiss authorities to keep abreast of the political developments in the international environment.

Specific institutional factors aggravate this further. The double majority rule in federal ballots (a proposition is accepted only if the majority of all voters *and* of all cantons support it) and the **bicameralism** of parliament privileges the small, rural cantons, most of whom are conservative. The small cantons have come to carry a disproportionately heavy political weight. Thus, for cantonal votes, one vote cast in the tiny Canton of Appenzell-Inner Rhodes influences the outcome 38 times more strongly than a vote cast in the populous, urbanized canton of Zurich. What was meant to be a federalist safeguard in 1848 is nowadays liable to block innovative legislation.

This is a rare paradox of the small exploiting the big. It occurs also within cantons. The Swiss system of locally assessed rates for certain major taxes has turned rich suburban and rural communes into freeriders. They are unwilling to help defray the high cost of infrastructure, services, and social welfare that urban centers face, yet they expect the central-place functions to benefit them as well. The ultimate caricature of Swiss federalism is the bank director in Zurich who jets to London during the day. There he finalizes a restructuring of the bank that will wipe out hundreds of jobs in the city. In the evening, he celebrates the deal with his wife joining him from their villa in Zumikon. Zumikon is a lakeside commune where his taxable has helped to lower the local rates, and his campaign donations have brought people to the cantonal parliament who vote down contributions for common welfare programs. The couple visit the opera and a restaurant, expecting the police to spare them the view of panhandlers and drug addicts—at the expense of the city taxpayers, among whom are bank employees headed for the unemployment office.

WEAK PARTIES, STRONG LOBBIES

The strength of the federalist and direct-democratic traditions in Switzerland makes for a weak state. The Swiss state is less autonomous vis-à-vis its ambient society than other, similarly small states in Western Europe. When the lines between state and powerful organized groups are so widely blurred, the latter become pseudo-governments. This necessitates a change of approach: We will deal with the recruiters of political decision makers—the political parties—and with the government's most important decision partners—the special-interest associations—*before* looking at the federal executive and legislative bodies. Another system that thrives between state and society—the **social movements**—will also be treated later in this chapter. For space reasons, only government institutions at the federal level will be analyzed.

The Party System: Fragmented Parties Produce Stable Governments

American students of politics are used to dealing with two-party systems, the best known being the Republicans and Democrats in the United States, who face each other in perpetual opposition and keep power alternating between them. Nothing could be more different from that than the political parties in Switzerland. We are dealing with a system that favors the coexistence of numerous parties. Its peculiarities begin right with their foundation history: The Swiss political parties have grown on the soil of direct democracy. They came into being as organizations meant to collect citizens' signatures for referenda and initiatives. This bottom-up growth explains why the parties have their homes and their strongest member identification in the cantons. For most parties, membership is with the local sections in the communes, and the cantonal chapters have retained large autonomy. New parties also originate in the cantons or even communes. They have the means to go national only when they have proven successful in a number of local arenas. In recent years, that has again been illustrated by the Swiss Ecological Party, a new party organized by members of a social movement. Moreover, new parties initially spread only to the large cantons where entry barriers set by the electoral system are comparatively low.

The number of parties that have survived from very diverse local origins is large. Kerr (1987) in a study of 23 democratic countries, found that only Finland and Israel counted more parties at the national level than Switzerland. In such a fractured system, the parties do still appeal to the masses (they are not exclusive political clubs), but their organizational structures are feeble. The annual budgets for the three major parties are in the magnitude of $1–1.5 million each (Kriesi 1995: 150; 1989 figures); subsidies by government are modest. The parties draw their greatest strength from the caliber of the people they recruit and promote.

Party leaders are typically upper-class persons: higher-echelon government employees for the **Social Democrats,** professionals in the conservative parties. The leaders tend to cumulate functions in other organizations that in turn strengthen the position of their parties. While participation in elections has been declining since 1935—we will come back to this later—eagerness to embark on a party career has not subsided at all. The number of candidates running for the federal parliament has more than doubled over the last 30 years. The growth of a well-educated middle class may be a principal reason for that.

Party fragmentation, surprisingly at first glance, has not led to government instability. The integrative forces of direct democracy have prevailed also on the party composition. In the federal arena, four parties have been sharing power, maintaining an identical composition of the top executive since 1959. The so-called Magic Formula lets two of the conservative parties and the Social-Democratic Party each hold two seats of the seven-seat **Federal Council.** One seat is always reserved for another conservative party. In that way, Switzerland has one of the most stable governments anywhere.

After the Magic Formula was founded in 1959, only one political party outside the ruling coalition (an atypical one at that, close to a powerful retailing chain) has had continuous, though modest, political success to be counted as an opposition force that mattered. This party, also remained ideologically close to the big parties. The moderate pluralism has since been challenged mainly by small parties on the extreme right of the spectrum, often aided by the People's Party.

Participation in federal elections and ballots has been declining since 1935. The voter turnout in National Assembly elections (a proportional election system based on party lists) fell from close to 80 percent in that year to around 45 percent in the late seventies, where it has leveled out. Swiss participation rates are thus considerably lower than election participation in neighboring countries, which have hovered around 75 percent. A decline, in the voters' eyes, of the importance of elections after the Magic Formula was institutionalized in 1959 has been offered as an explanation.

Special-Interest Associations:
The Seats of Power

An important fact of Swiss politics is the historical lead that powerful interest associations have had over political parties. The national organization of business in the second half of the 19th century predated the appearance of political parties at the federal level by some 20 years. The subsidiarity principle, placing private initiative above government intervention, was one of the values professed by those **capitalist** milieux. Later, when government activity grew massively, other, sometimes hidden, factors worked for the special-interest associations. The top executive body in federal government, as we shall see, has a relatively weak position, allowing a shift of power to the federal bureaucracy. This in turn enhances the role that the bureaucracy's implementing partners, the **special-interest associations,** play in politics. In Switzerland, the associations negotiate with government on equal footing, and they do so in the legislative as well as in the implementing phases. We look in some depth at the business associations and the trade unions, the most important associational groupings in the political process.

Business Associations:
The Government's Strongest Partners

When the Federal Office of Industry, Business and Employment surveyed its list of partner organizations in 1986, it found 1,116 with whom it had regular dealings (Kriesi 1995: 225). No fewer than 675, or 60 percent, of those were business associations. For a small country, that is a lot. Most of the numerous business associations belong to one of four major apex organizations:

- Swiss Association of Small Businesses.
- The so-called Vorort, the tandem office of the Swiss Association of Commerce and Industry (representing above all the export-oriented industries) and the Central Association of Swiss Employers' Organizations.
- Swiss Bankers' Association.
- Swiss Farmers' Association.

These associations have known to avoid the fragmentation that is plaguing the political parties. The Commerce and Industry, and Employers associations developed a comprehensive matrix structure on regional as well as sectoral criteria. The Employers Association is particularly strong, representing 72 percent of all employers in the business sector (the nonorganized are generally very small businesses). Over the years, these two associations have become the government's strongest partners in matters of economic policy.

The business associations have been key in creating and maintaining the peculiar coexistence in Switzerland of economic sectors working for domestic markets but highly protected from foreign competition versus other industries that compete aggressively in the world market. Together with the state, who ratified their rules of competition, the associations are responsible for the highly protected nature of much of Swiss business. The economic structure shaped by the government–association nexus has had tremendous consequences, and these have gone far beyond economics and politics. Protected and **cartellized** markets saved producers from being wiped out by competition over price. The protection helped to consolidate Swiss society toward a very broad middle class. Competition acted itself out over the quality of goods, helped by the stream of techno-logical innovations in the export-led sectors. High-quality goods in turn helped to modernize cultural icons important for the Swiss identity. Pro-tected markets also created political and economic fiefs that are the soil and nurture of the traditionalist forces. The business associations have had far-reaching effects; their activities cannot be summed up simply as lobbying for distributional gains. More than that, they have, in alliance with the state, created social structure.

Trade Unions: Faltering Guarantors of Industrial Peace

The workers and employee trade unions may be considered the natural antagonists of the business organizations or, as in the dominant Swiss credo, their partners of special confidence. What is certain, however, is that the trade union movement in Switzerland has not matched orga-nized business in internal coherence and membership strength. It inher-ited the ideological rift between the socialist milieux of the Protestant cantons and the Catholic migrants from conservative rural cantons. Sev-eral subsystems have formed, on philosophical or on industry sector bases. Overall membership has been decreasing since 1977 when the Confederation introduced a mandatory unemployment insurance scheme (thus removing the incentive to belong to the optional schemes that the trade unions were operating for their members); in 1986, 27 per-cent of the active population were union members, a development that lumps Switzerland together with major industrial countries like Japan, the United States, and France, who all have seen union strength falter since the Second World War. The global figure conceals important sec-toral changes that the Swiss economy is undergoing in its transformation toward a stronger service sector.

Thus, between 1980 and 1990, the textile workers' unions suffered membership decline in pace with their contracting employment while the media workers' union, an assertive sector, grew by 63 percent in membership. In sum, the trade unions each benefit more from richer re-sources and strong centralization than do the political parties. But they are also undoubtedly much weaker than the organized capitalist inter-ests. A structural asymmetry exists between the two, rich in conse-quences for the political process. It is little perceived, though, because of the social partnership that business and unions have been cultivating since the late thirties. This deserves a miniature historical *aperçu*.

Like other capitalist countries, Switzerland entered the 20th century with a highly polarized class structure. Social tensions exploded at the end of the First World War in a general strike, which was put down under military threat. Tensions resumed gravely during the protracted economic crisis in the thirties while the country was sandwiched between powerful fascist regimes manifestly heading for war. Internal dissension became a question of national survival. Under the threat of government intervention, a collective convention was signed in 1937 between the Metal Workers and Watchmakers Union and the corresponding employers association. It obligated the partners to the principles of good faith and peaceful relations and introduced binding arbitration of disputes. Strikes and lockouts were prohibited. In time, collective conventions were concluded in all major industries and service sectors. Industrial relations since then have been self-regulated. The employers contribute financially to the social activities and overhead costs of the trade unions. These in turn help to maintain a disciplined and well-trained workforce. At the end of the Second World War—remember, Switzerland was spared hostilities in both wars—the transition was managed without great social antagonism. This, together with the unscathed production apparatus and monetary regime, allowed Switzerland to cash in the political stability rent that would fuel unparalleled economic and social growth until the seventies.

No wonder, then, that the trade unions, despite their weakness in the face of the more strongly organized business associations, are counted as strong actors in Swiss politics. Kriesi (1980), in a study of the most important political decision processes in the seventies, asked members of the political elite to rate the influence of the special-interest associations against that of other actors. By and large, the associations, together with the cantons, were credited with a strong, if not dominant, influence, sometimes matched, seldom surpassed, by that of the federal cabinet and its administration. The political parties and the parliament stood virtually eclipsed.

ORGANS OF GOVERNMENT: PARLIAMENT AND CABINET

We have passed through the netherlands of Swiss society, crossed the rivers that divide it, and hiked over the hills of organized interests. Now we are prepared for the final ascent onto the mountain of formal political institutions. Already familiar with the terrain, we do not expect to climb a towering peak, but only a modest rise from the rest of the panorama.

The Swiss federal constitution defines three major institutions. The **Federal Assembly** may be approximated to Congress in the American terminology. The cabinet level of government is called the **Federal Council**. The supreme judicial authority is vested in the *Federal Tribunal*. However, it does not have jurisdiction over the constitutionality of laws. As such, its political significance is limited, and we shall not dwell on the judicial branch of government. The legislative branch clearly dominates among the three, but this finding is modified by the weight of the federal administration.

The Federal Assembly: Rubberstamping What Happened in the Lobby?

The Federal Assembly is the supreme authority of the **Confederation.** It follows a perfect **bicameralism,** copying the United States example, with the difference that the two chambers have equal powers. Every bill has to be passed by both. The **National Council** seats 200 members elected on party lists in proportion to their popular vote. Importantly, each canton is a circumscription. In small cantons, national councilors are therefore elected in a de-facto majoritarian system. The Swiss system is very different from those of some other countries. For example, in the Netherlands, the whole country forms one big electoral district. The **Council of States** assembles 46 representatives of the cantons. They are elected by popular vote, not—as in Germany—appointed by the state governments. Their electoral mode is majoritarian and regulated by cantonal laws. Most cantons send two councilors. Six cantons, for historic reasons, are counted as half-cantons, entitled to one councilor only.

The work capacity of parliament is extended by 10 permanent commissions. The most powerful ones are the Commission on Foreign Policy; the Commission of the Economy and Taxes, which looks into fiscal policy; and the Finance Commission, which strengthens budget making and control. While the commissions are important, with the dominant conservative parties taking many of the chairs, preparliamentary procedures, as explained in the section on direct democracy, carry a far greater weight than the parliamentary phase does. When a problem is accepted on the federal political agenda, generally draft legislation is worked out by the administration or by independent experts. Extensive consultations with the cantons, political parties, interest associations, and issue groups follow. One of the objectives is to prepare a compromise version for parliamentary debate that minimizes the risk of a referendum being taken when a bill is passed (or, in matters that entail mandatory referenda, minimize the risk of defeat by the popular vote). Positions in the preparliamentary commissions, while including politically neutral experts from the administration and academia, are primarily polarized along the left–right dimension; and it is on that note that their work is discussed in the public. The ability to reach compromise has declined since the seventies, as the greater use of the optional referendum attests.

The referendum threat is not the only factor that limits the influence of parliament. Switzerland does not know the vote of no-confidence (nor can the government dissolve parliament). It is the Federal Council that largely sets the pace at which the various legislative projects can advance and can selectively adopt elements of the political agenda. If parliament does not agree with the Federal Council's procedural policies, it has no direct sanction.

Moreover, the Federal Assembly is not a professional parliament. Theoretically, and looking only at the modest support they receive, members are volunteers; practically they are semiprofessionals. Parliamentary services employ only about 50 people, a number magnitudes smaller than the 1,700 staffers of the German Bundestag, let alone the 20,000 of the American Congress (Riklin and Möckli 1990).

The same authors have called the Swiss parliament "little enterprising and even extremely timid." Among the many bills that are proposed by parliamentarians, most concern updates and modifications of existing laws; their innovative content is low, in contrast to popular initiatives, which usually respond to a burning problem. Members of parliament have tried to enhance the political impulses from their ranks, but the adoption rate for their projects dropped drastically. The political elite themselves are frank about the fact that the preparliamentary phases are more decisive, with the exception of urgency measures that the government has the parliament approve in crisis situations. If parliament retains its important place in the process, it is because every group attempts to have the bills modified in its favor.

Note that the legislative process in Switzerland is slow. The median delay between the first formal impulsion and the publication of a new law in the government gazette is around three years (Poitry 1989). Three-quarters of that time is spent in preparliamentary deliberations. Formal procedures in parliament take up 14 percent of the gestation time, while the referendum phase—the collection of signatures for an optional referendum, as well as the run-up to the ballot—accounts for 12 percent of the life of legislative projects. The legislative inertia bodes ill for new situations that demand speed and adaptability, notably in European integration challenges.

There is an apparent contradiction between the high esteem in which the Swiss hold their authorities and the lack of resources to which they have condemned their Federal Assembly. Nor has the Swiss democracy been able, or even willing, to limit extraparliamentary influence. The current system favors the direct representation of special interests over principled debate. The formal functions of the Swiss parliament appear like a thin film of cheese sandwiched between the heavy slices of the preparlimentary process and the referendum fight.

The Federal Council: Exceptional Continuity

The executive branch of the Swiss government is modeled after the **French Revolution** government of 1795. This was a directorial system, and it meant that a small number of executives were elected by parliament to work as a body of peers for the coordination of overall government policy and for the supervision of the specialized ministries. During their tenure they were not politically responsible to the parliament that elected them. In Switzerland, this body is known as the Federal Council. It is composed of seven members of equal standing. The chairmanship among the seven Federal Councilors rotates annually; the chairperson is at the same time president of the Swiss Confederation. The president remains a peer with his fellow Federal Councilors;

the directorial system does not admit the kind of executive presidency with all its power and prestige that the United States has developed so prominently. In fact, many Swiss would not know the current president of the Confederation. The media do cover the annual ritual of the parliament electing the new president, but it is by all means not an event of great national importance.

The emphasis is not on outstanding personalities but on institutional continuity. Almost all Federal Councilors in the history of modern Switzerland have been reelected as long as they personally stood again. Since 1848, there has never been a change of government involving the complete renewal of the Federal Council. And, as we mentioned earlier, the famous Magic Formula has kept the political party composition of the seven members exactly the same since 1959.

Additional informal rules want two members of the Federal Council to be French speakers. The largest among the cantons also make claims to Council seats. Care is taken to balance the Catholic and Protestant denominations, and in the nineties perfunctory respect is being paid to women. Accommodating all the demands on the composition of the Federal Council often comes at the expense of the competence of its members. Also it tends to prevent the government from elaborating and following coherent political programs.

The Federal Council has a key position above all as a mediator in the political process. The councilors, as a small peer group, mutually control the draft legislation prepared jointly by various government departments. To a large degree, the Council sets the pace at which the various projects advance in the decision-making process. As it can be neither dismissed by parliament nor challenged in a constitutional court, it enjoys far-reaching autonomy.

The Federal Council's major limitation is its workload. Each member supervises a conglomerate of functions that in other countries are shared between a larger number of ministries. With the growth of government and the greater urgency of many matters in a harsher economic climate, the Federal Council has become dysfunctionally overburdened. As a result, power has shifted toward the federal administration, and the kind of high-level policy deliberation that the French Revolutionary directorate model assigned to the Federal Council has largely been replaced by coordination between departments at lower echelons.

ELITE AND CHALLENGERS

The Swiss Political Elite: The Marriage of Politics, Economy and the Military

Swiss democracy is intensive in coordination. The cantons need to be listened to carefully, and the special-interest groups are heavily consulted. The coordination is ensured by a political elite whose workings are not very well known due to their preference for closed-door negotiations. The

TABLE 16

Most Politically Powerful Organizations in Switzerland

Rank	Organization
1	Association of Swiss Trade Unions
2	Swiss Association of Commerce and Industry
3	Swiss Association of Small Businesses
4	Federal Council
5	Swiss Farmers Association
6	Christian Democratic Party
7	Liberal-Democratic Party
8	Social Democratic Party
9	Swiss National Bank
10	Federal Department of the Economy
11	Federal Department of Finance
12	Federal Office of Foreign Economic Affairs
13	Association of Swiss Health Care Insurance Providers
14	Central Association of Swiss Employers Organizations
15	Federal Office of Industry, Small Business and Employment
16	Federal Administration of Finance

Source: Hanspeter Kriesi, *Entscheidungsstrukturen und Entscheidungsprozesse in der Schweizer Politik* (Frankfurt: Campus, 1980), p. 316.

power configuration was studied in the seventies by Kriesi (1980), who identified an inner circle of 300 powerful individuals belonging to 170 organizations and government departments. The center of an intensive cooperation network was held by 16 core-power organizations (see Table 16) of whom 11 exercised influence in several policy domains, the others being more specialized.

A more detailed analysis of how the elite members cooperated in different policy domains modified those insights somewhat. At the hub of the power network, the Federal Council held the reins, closely surrounded by the most important offices of the federal administration, the Liberal Democratic Party, and key business associations. But there were specialized areas such as health care and land zoning policy in which the left—the Social Democrats and trade unions—had considerable influence. The elite cooperation networks seemed to be demarcated primarily between social and economic policy areas. The inner circle was, and is, essentially composed of conservative politicians. The left is strongly integrated, but in a clear minority position.

Looking at the social background of the individuals who lead those powerful organizations, we will, after all, not be surprised to find vast differences in comparison with the Swiss population at large. Members of the Federal Assembly were 6 times more likely to be business owners or top managers, 12 times more likely to belong to a classical profession (lawyers!), and 14 times more likely to be senior government administrators, professors, or clergy than ordinary folks (Kerr 1981). Although Kerr's data are now over 15 years old, nothing indicates that the professional background of parliamentarians has significantly changed. Women have risen slowly to Federal Assembly positions, from a mere 5 percent of all elected to 17 percent during the 20-year period 1971–91 (Federal Office of Statistics 1993a: 71). This is not particularly out of line with other European countries. However, and this is important for the national coherence of Switzerland, the political elite are well balanced on language and regional criteria.

It is trivial, after all that we know, that the councilors of the conservative parties work primarily for business and farmers, whereas many parliamentarians of the left belong to the world of trade unions. An excellent indicator of extraparliamentary influence cumulation is supplied by the number of seats that councilors hold in the boardrooms of various public and private organizations. Over the past 15 years, members from all parties have garnered a growing number of such offices. Interparty differences are extremely important. The average Christian Democrat among the federal parliamentarians during the period 1987–91 ran up a handsome 9.7 boardroom seats. Social Democrats, mostly limited to public sector influence, had to be content with an average of 2.6 mandates. The more director positions councilors heap up, the less time, in general, they have to give for parliamentary work. Councilors who are lawyers are particularly successful in expanding their extraparliamentary influence, with some of them raking in well over 20 director seats (Kriesi 1995: 194).

I have underlined the interpenetration between politics and economics. Another elite characteristic is the personal involvement of the conservative politicians (already close to business) in the officer corps of the Swiss army. Thus, about 40 percent of the various conservative party member of the 1987–91 Federal Assembly were officers in the Swiss army, as against only 7 percent of the Social Democratic parliamentarians (6 percent of all servicemen are officers). The strong correlation vindicates those who see the army as a network facilitating advancement in, and reinforcing cohesion among, the political and economic elite.

The Swiss elite are a power elite in the sense of C. Wright Mills (1956). The inner circles of the economic, political, and military elites overlap considerably. But the instruments of direct democracy allow the governed to challenge the elite rule in the political realm. Many such challenges have been mounted by **social movements** not yet well integrated into the political system, and to these I now turn.

Social Movements: Challengers Today, Partners Tomorrow

The year 1968 was a watershed year for political life in Switzerland as well as in other Western European countries. An explosion of protest, which would peak around 1973, brought massive discontent, particularly among the young, to the fore. While the protests could not dislodge the ruling-party coalition, they opened a field for extraparliamentary opposition. New social movements have since remained active, surpassing the traditional themes pursued by the workers' movement. They mobilized individuals and groups concerned with the ecology, peace, the Third World, the situation of women, urban low-cost housing, and other issues. From the mid-seventies onward, traditionalist social movements also have formed, rallying particularly those who see themselves threatened by the global economic transformations.

The reaction of the authorities toward the new social movements was at first to associate them with the communist threat. But over the years more differentiated forms of coexistence have evolved. The political elite could not fail to note that certain movements— for example, the ecology movement—enjoyed large support in the population. But the key in bringing both sides closer is again found in the openness of the political system through the institutions of direct democracy. Because direct democracy uses peaceful means outside elections in order to change elite agendas and decisions, it reduces the cost of individual participation in social movements. It thus has a mobilizing effect. Kriesi, Koopmans, Duyvordak, and Giugni (1995a) calculated a mobilization index based on various forms of political activities per million inhabitants for four democracies. Switzerland outranked the Netherlands, Germany, and France by far. During the 15-year period that they studied, the average Swiss person took part in 2.3 social movement events. In the nondirect democracy with the strongest movements, the Netherlands, the corresponding figure was only 0.7. At the same time, direct democracy moderates the movements. For that Switzerland offers two indicators. Here, as in other European countries, membership in environmental protection groups recorded strong growth throughout the 80s. Some groups were more radical than others. The most radical of all, Greenpeace, grew dramatically in the Netherlands and in Germany, but remained relatively insignificant in Switzerland. Second, violence and confrontation were less frequent in Switzerland than, say, in France with her centralist and authoritarian traditions. Kriesi and others (1995a) were able to calculate the rate of violent and confrontational events in the social movement repertoires. Table 17 evidences the relationship between type of democracy and social movement behavior.

In addition to their overt function—innovating on the political agenda—social movements have several latent ones. They are a training ground for ordinary citizens in organizational skills and politics and, to the extent that a movement becomes integrated in mainstream politics, also recruiters for new political elite members. They also promote cultural and social change. The women's movement comes to mind, with its struggle to better the position of women also in families, education, and the economy.

Direct democracy and the social movements, therefore, have to be seen together in Switzerland. They have not been able to unseat the rule

TABLE 17

Social Movement Strength in Various Democracies

Type of Democracy and Country	Mobilization (participation per million people)	Violence and confrontation
Direct: Switzerland	2,289,000	25.8%
Representative: Netherlands	712,000	46.1
Representative: Germany	608,000	34.5
Representative: France	535,000	55.7

Note: The data are for the entire period 1975 through 1989.

Source: Hanspeter Kriesi, *Le Système Politique Suisse* (Paris: Ed. Economica, 1995).

of the conservative elite (in fact, as we have seen, together with the federalist structure, direct democracy has in part helped to entrench the conservatives), but they have introduced an element of unpredictability that keeps the elite on its toes. They make it easier for the citizenry to escape from the control by its politicians.

IS SWISS GOVERNMENT BY CONSENSUS UNIQUE?

At the same time, one has to put the place and effects of the Swiss democratic system in perspective. It would be wrong to think that Switzerland was the only European democracy with a strong tendency to adopt political opposition groups into governing coalitions. Similar behaviors have been noted for other small countries, notably the Netherlands, Norway, Sweden and Austria. These countries do not have a tradition of direct democracy, which therefore cannot be the sole force working for political integration. Katzenstein (1985) was the first to suggest that the size of the country might be a factor as decisive as political tradition in favoring integrative regimes. His argument is appealing because it ties national politics to global economic change: Small countries are more vulnerable, socially and economically, to changes in the world markets. Political systems that rely on broad coalitions help to absorb the economic shocks because they create in society a commitment and flexibility for the necessary adaptations. Close cooperation between government, employers, and trade unions is the cornerstone of such a strategy. Tripartite arrangements go back to the years of economic crisis in the 1930s. The large European countries, who were then similarly hard hit, were not able to develop broad and stable coalitions because of their authoritarian state traditions and the violence that radicalized the workers' movement.

For the last two decades, however, Katzenstein would have a hard time proving that the Swiss political system has greatly helped the kind of flexibility that world market changes demand of small countries. It has not delivered on integration with Europe. But after the inclusion in government of the Catholic and linguistic minorities in the 19th century and of the farm-ers, and workers, movement in the 20th century, something else happened: Strong economic growth and the delegation of lowly jobs to foreigners dur-ing the period 1945–1975 consolidated the majority of the Swiss in an un-usually prosperous middle class. The federalist system and protection of important sectors from foreign competition subsidized a large number of fiefs in the public as well as private sectors. In combination, they removed incentives for big change in the political system. Why change while the sys-tem keeps the elite and most of the voters warm and fed? Kriesi thinks that the coziness may not go on for long. In the nineties, voter satisfaction is de-creasing; confidence in government is declining. He likens the current situ-ation to the one that prevailed immediately before the fall of the old Switzerland at the end of the 18th century (Kriesi 1995: 223). But at that time, it took the invasion by the French Revolutionary armies to overthrow the regime. It is as yet impossible to see the contours of a major disaster that could deal a similar blow to a modern Switzerland attached, as it is, to its traditions of federalism, neutrality, and direct democracy.

CONCLUSION

Inertia is the keyword to characterize the Swiss political system. In the beginning of the chapter, I referred to the "freezing" hypothesis, mean-ing that the party systems of several European countries in the sixties re-flected the social conditions at the end of the First World War, 50 years earlier. But only Switzerland has been able to repeat this feat, harboring to this date a coalition government that has been in place, in its almost identical party composition, since 1943. In the meantime, of course, Swiss society and the world have not remained static. The political con-stituency is nowadays dominated by a much broader and better edu-cated middle class than at the time when the Social Democrats were inducted to government responsibility as the last in a series of major op-position groups. Political differences have become complicated beyond the earlier simple **left (socialist)–right** (**liberal** and **conservative** in Swiss parlance) opposition, with a new polarity growing stronger between **cos-mopolitan** and **traditionalist** forces.

This new constellation also affects the way in which the principal traditions of Swiss politics are being continued. We have seen that **direct democracy,** with its twin instruments of **initiative** and **referendum,** cre-ated a culture of accommodation and compromise that pervades all of Swiss political life, but can also stand in the way of major innovations. The key instance of this inhibitory effect in recent history concerned closer links with the **European Union,** which the government pursued, but the people vetoed. **Neutrality** has become an even more firmly be-sieged principle in politics. Not only are the Swiss divided among them-selves as to how to interpret neutrality in the face of multinational organizations such as the **United Nations** through which Switzerland needs to assert its influence abroad. Also the international community, having a new look at 20th-century history after the Cold War has ended, is less forgiving about Swiss business with the powers of the Second World War and with its contemporary isolationism, both justified in the name of its neutrality. Compared to direct democracy and neutrality, **federalism** finds the most favorable philosophical climate for its continuation. Domestically, it is the key mechanism for the peaceful coexistence of several cultural groups. Internationally, it is in good standing because several other Western democracies, including Germany and the United States, have federalist systems. The downside is that federalism disperses political power in a time when economic power is being concentrated and, in Switzerland, gives too much of it to the smaller cantons, who also happen to be the more rural and traditionalist ones, thus putting an additional brake on innovation and adaptability.

The net result of the Swiss political traditions, since the inception of the modern federal state in 1848, has been a weak state. That does not mean a poorly performing government machinery. Rather, the state is weak because direct democracy and federalism fling it wide open to the influence of the ambient society. Cabinet and parliament, while not unimportant, look smallish and discolored vis-à-vis the thousand cogs and wheels of the bureaucracy, the power of the special-interest organizations, and the motley whirl and swirl of social movements. The weakness of the state admittedly has made it permeable for new issues and demands and as such has been instrumental for the peace and cohesiveness that Swiss society has enjoyed for so long. But its ability to legislate solutions for major problems in an era of worldwide, rapid, and deep change is seriously in doubt.

FURTHER READING

Linder, Wolf. *Swiss Democracy. Possible Solutions to Conflict in Multicultural Societies.* New York: St. Martin's Press, 1994. An analysis of the contribution that the major instruments of Swiss direct democracy have made to national stability.

CHAPTER 5

Switzerland in the World Economy

*F*ew *Americans face the decision to do their weekend grocery shopping in Canada or Mexico, or in any other foreign country. Yet, when I lived in Geneva, my friends, together with droves of other Swiss, would hop the border to buy meat, butter, and other cheap items in nearby French supermarkets, passing under the vigilant eyes of customs agents. Their attention was distracted from drugs, illegal immigrants, and firearms by their zeal to make sure that we did not exceed the allowance of one kilogram of meat per person or any other quotas. The amazing price differentials with neighbors with whom Switzerland trades extensively is but one manifestation of a very special economic situation. This was created over the entire period since the industrial revolution; and it is being preserved by the strong association between the state, business, and labor.*

Modern Swiss economic history has maneuvered between two poles. Switzerland is, in economic terms, a middle-sized power. At the same time, its economy has had to make the kinds of adaptations that the world market imposes on small countries. This means, for example, that Switzerland does not have the clout to found entirely new industries; it has not had a hand in creating the modern computer. But the country has excelled in building on some of its old export industries and moving into technologically related areas. Pharmaceuticals is the best, and best known, of the success stories of that kind, but there are more. The intent of this chapter is to show the consequences for economic success of peace and stability, of the small country situation, as well as of specialization and technological competence. A brief characterization of the three basic sectors—agriculture, manufacturing and construction, and services—is also given. Problems of adapting to the fast-changing world economy are raised, and critical linkages between economy and society are suggested.

DOMESTIC AND EXPORT:
A DOUBLE-FACED ECONOMY

A Wealthy People

By 1994, per capita income was about $24,000 at purchasing power parity, making the Swiss the fourth wealthiest people. Ahead of Switzerland, ranked in descending order, were Luxembourg, the United States and Kuwait, and next behind were Hong Kong, Singapore, and Japan ("The Great Debate" 1996: 6). Growth to those heights took place within the framework created by the **factor endowment** of Switzerland, but also by its institutional conditions and political stability. The country is poor in natural resources and does not produce enough food. Incentives have therefore been strong since early on in modernization to expand foreign trade and to sell more abroad in order to buy more abroad. Significant foreign trade began in the 13th century when mountain herdsmen found buyers in the populous cities of northern Italy for their meat, skins, and wool—and for their cheese, a highlight of the Swiss export industry to this day. Export incentives were reinforced by the small domestic market for industrial goods; exports from a centrally located country created economies of scale fast. Those basic conditions were in place already during the industrialization of the 19th century. In the 20th century, it is its extraordinary political stability that earned Switzerland a strong economic premium. The country was unscathed by the two world wars and by hyperinflation; its banks attracted very large foreign deposits. For many decades, capital was cheaper than in most other Western European countries. Terms were uniquely favorable for Switzerland. The small country built a daunting international competitiveness thanks to capital-intensive research, development, and manufacturing. Long-term investment was not only in plant and machinery and in research and development, but also in manpower competent in the skills needed in each firm. Wages grew more slowly than total productivity, and the labor force was expanded through immigration. At the same time the economy boosted its capital intensity and specialization in niches where it drew **quasi-monopolistic** rents. Over time, the abundance of cheap capital became self-reinforcing. Swiss investors placed large fortunes abroad; returns on such investments together with income from services has given Switzerland continuous current-account surpluses that have strengthened its international position, kept the capital markets awash, and financed its chronic trade balance deficit. A graphic indicator of that strength, Swiss per capita investment abroad is the highest of all countries, six times the respective US value (Kriesi 1995: 29).

The institutional framework is less easy to characterize. Formally, Switzerland has a liberal capitalist market economy. Its constitution guarantees the right to property and economic freedom. The actual importance of the private sector confirms that view. Switzerland, if we look at the share of government expenditure in the national product—the

TABLE 18

Economic Importance of Government

Country	Government Quota
Japan	30%
Switzerland	*35*
USA	35
Germany	44
Sweden	65

*This is the percentage of government expenditure in the gross national product (GNP). The GNP, a measure of a countries total economic activity during one year, is a complex figure. It is composed of the consumption of private households, businesses, and the government; the export surplus; capitol and labor incomes from abroad; as well as the subsidies minus indirect taxes.

Note: Data are for 1992.

Source: Beat Hotz-Hart, Stefan Maeder, and Patrick Vock, *Volkswirtschaft der Schweiz* (Zurich: vdf Hockschulverlag AG an der ETH Zurich, 1995), p. 487.

government quota—holds a place similar to that of the United States, slightly above Japan's, and way below Germany's, let alone Sweden's with its heavy redistribution by government (see Table 18).

Other indicators, also place Switzerland in the group of very liberal economies. For example, Swiss labor law affords workers less protection from layoffs than Germany and some northern European countries do. In Germany, labor representatives have mandatory seats on the boards of directors of major companies, an arrangement that Switzerland has not followed. On the other hand, working citizens (and others) are protected under a well-developed social security and welfare system. Unemployment insurance is mandatory. So is health insurance, but the premium is usually paid by the beneficiary.

A Liberal Economy Not of the Textbook Variety

Yet we are dealing with a kind of double-faced economy that is very different from the textbook market economy. The political regulation of the market is far-reaching in Switzerland. It works not so much by detailed government intervention, but rather by official sanction of self-regulation that limits competition. The close interaction between organized economic interests and political institutions makes regulation easier.

Branches with a primarily domestic orientation are safeguarded against competition, particularly from abroad. Conversely, export-oriented firms operate in international markets that do not provide them political protection. Domestically oriented businesses often are farmers, small and medium-sized manufacturers, retailers, and construction firms. Part of the banking sector does most of its business at home. Some of the very large economic organizations with a domestic orientation are government **monopolies:** the postal services, railroads, and electricity companies. The importance of small and medium-sized firms—localists and exporters alike—is multidimensional: Firms with fewer than 500 employees account for 75 percent of all employment. The Swiss Small Business Association is politically powerful; these firms have their own culture. It emphasizes quality and reliability, and long-term and emotionally rewarding relationships with customers, suppliers, workers, and officials. It de-emphasizes competition. A Swiss lawyer advertises once in her professional life: when she opens her practice. From then on it's word of mouth.

Sectors with a primary orientation toward export are often dominated by large enterprises that bring the critical mass to stand up in the international markets. Thus, concentration in the banking sector in Switzerland is much stronger than in Germany with her vast domestic business. The three largest institutes in Switzerland do 43 percent of all banking business (and will soon do much more, due to a megafusion in 1998); their three giant brothers in Germany control around 10 percent only.

As most firms are members in the comprehensive system of business associations, many product markets are highly **cartellized.** In a pun on Adam Smith's famous invisible hand of the market, Hotz-Hart, Maeder, and Vock (1995: 71) wryly note that "the visible hand of the state in Switzerland influences . . . almost two thirds of all prices." Some factor markets are thereby also controlled, notably the labor market. Collective conventions on employment determine the price of labor to a large extent. Although exact surveys do not exist, it may be reasonably supposed that to this day Switzerland is one of the countries with the highest cartel density. Another indicator of the extent of protection emerges from the Swiss external trade dependency. The Swiss ratio is similar to that of some other small European countries, but is by no means the highest among this group. In other words, the Swiss are not yet relying on imported products and semi-products as much as the more open economies do; their protective regime enables greater manufacturing depth at home.

Cartel costs are enormous. They are paid chiefly by consumers and government. It has been estimated that in the jungle of federalist tendering and procurement systems, prices are on average 50 percent above those of a fully competitive market. The annual volume of government orders is in the tune of $20 billion or 10 percent of the gross domestic product. You may estimate from those percentages that roughly 3 percent of the value of all domestic activity goes as a free gift to the business partners of the federalist system. Add to that the rents levied on the annual $150 billion household consumption, and you understand that the politically regulated economy has built fortresses of vested interests around it.

The Noneconomic Consequences of Protection

The protected economy has important noneconomic consequences. The conservative elements in politics and economy reinforce each other. The key values in Swiss economic policy are the ones that govern private economics: stability, continuity, predictability. Policy looks backward, trying above all to conserve structure. It is slow, sometimes slothful, self-critical only on a perfunctory note. A primary example is the growth of farm subsidies (see also below). With farming particularly important in the small cantons, who can block federal legislation by special majority requirements, economy and politics are essentially paying for their mutual deadlock.

Yet the domestically oriented sector is not closed. It works in harmony with the export-led industries. Cartellization has not manifestly hampered technological innovation, supplier concentration, and productivity growth. It is competition over quality that is often the driving force for modernization. One surmises that the quality and technological requirements of the export industries are passed on to their suppliers, whence they spread to the economy at large. The quality of goods in general and of many services is above international average. This leads to a somewhat paradoxical situation: Individual firms adapt technologically to the world market. At the same time they stay members of a branch **cartel,** or subject to government regulations that limit competition in their factor and product markets.

In previous chapters, we noted a two-dimensional cleavage in modern Swiss politics. It has a strong basis in the duality of the Swiss economy. The traditional left–right antagonism historically goes back to distributional conflict between labor and capital. The more recent opposition between traditionalist and cosmopolitan forces is inspired notably by the different world views that the regulated domestically oriented and the export-led sectors encourage. We may illustrate the point with the two extremes on this dimension.

The city of Basle has for a long time been home to cultural liberalism. While Protestantism, urbanity, and close neighborhood with Germany and France all have their share in forming the Basle outlook, part of the reason is the dominant Basle industry, chemicals and pharmaceuticals, with its ethos of service to distant and alien customers and its quest for discovery and invention. For the mountain farmer in central Switzerland, the situation is entirely different. His paycheck comes from the milk-marketing cooperative to which he supplies government-regulated quantities at government-regulated prices. His milk may eventually be turned into one of the world's best cheeses and sold in a New York delicatessen. But it is the Swiss Cheese Association that decides the formula and the label. If he doesn't like that, or does not like the way the association is run, he should think twice. The Basle habit of writing rebellious letters to newspaper editors may not be helpful for survival in his situation. Yet he will probably never see his cooperative close down, too deeply are these farm interests entrenched in politics. Not so for his brother, a worker in a pharmaceutical factory in Basle. If liberal attitudes lead to stricter animal rights laws, he may find himself unemployed, the factory moved to another country with more business-friendly regulations. The cultural effects of duality will become even clearer when we consider the effects of specialization in the next section.

Strong Ties with Foreign Countries

The export-oriented sector has created intense connectivity with the economies of the rest of the world. Switzerland has one of the highest densities of multinational corporations among all nations. For example, for every million population, Switzerland hosts the headquarters of 436 such entities. The United States boasts 12. In other words, the density for Switzerland is 35 times that for the United States. For foreign affiliates of multinationals, the Swiss figures are similarly staggering (see Table 19). These are telling characteristics of a small, but rich country.

Another constant in the Swiss economic equation deserves brief mention here. That is the strong orientation toward Germany. Europe absorbs about two-thirds of the Swiss exports, not a surprise for a land-locked country in the heart of the continent. Germany is a particularly important partner. In 1994, 23 percent of all goods exported went there; of all imported, no less than 33 percent were bought from Germany. With German growth flattening under the burden of unification after 1989, the Swiss economy also is set for a slower pace. The dependency is not without cultural ambiguity. The Swiss acknowledge that Germany is the economic steam engine in Europe. From the time of the Second World War, they have also kept an uneasiness about the growing power of their northern neighbor. Again, the ramifications are more than just economic: In the German-speaking part of Switzerland, the pronounced use of local dialects is a deliberate means to mark Swiss distinctiveness.

TABLE 19

Density of Multinationals for Various Countries

Country	Parent Corporations	Foreign Affiliates
Switzerland	436	582
Germany (West)	109	184
Holland	96	135
Japan	29	26
United States	12	60

Note: Manufacturing and services, per million population.

Source: Calculated after "The Discreet Charm of the Multicultural Multinational," *The Economist,* June 30, 1994, p. 60.

STAKEHOLDER VALUE: MIGROS

Do you need a new vacuum cleaner? Would natural rice be good for your diet? Does your girlfriend love those fresh orchids from Sri Lanka? Does your family want a vacation in Spain? Studying up on your French? Need gas? Ever thought of life insurance?—"Migros has got it" for you.

Migros is a household word with every Swiss and a specific way of doing business that pursues a range of objectives, capitalist and others. On the surface, Migros, for short, is a retailing chain with national coverage. It holds a 16 percent market share in all retailing and, after the government-owned postal and telephone services, is the second biggest employer in the country, with 72,000 workers. But essentially, Migros is a state within the state. Established in 1925 by a charismatic entrepreneur and transformed into a cooperative in 1941, it is a conglomerate run on modern business lines as well as a multifaceted social and cultural institution.

One in every two Swiss households is a member of a regional Migros cooperative. Membership carries no financial benefits or discounts, but members receive the weekly *Bridge Builder* magazine with a wealth of consumer and general educational information. In fact, the money Migros makes in tending to the needs of our bodies seems but a pretext for educating a prosperous society at large. More than half of all adult education classes in Switzerland are taken in Migros clubs. Another aspect of its reformist philosophy is in the fact that Migros does not sell alcohol or tobacco. The charter mandates that 1 percent of the retailing turnover be spent for cultural purposes, which has made Migros one of the major supporters of Swiss movies, concerts, and art collections. Differently from normal sponsoring, its name more often than not remains untold. It also pays for the Gottlieb Duttweiler Institute, a think tank on social and economic questions, and is affiliated with one of the small opposition parties. At the other end of Swiss society, in remote rural areas, "Migros wagons," rolling small retail outlets, sell groceries to the elderly and other people unable to do shopping in towns. Less well known by the public, but equally pertinent to its broad economic and social charter, the Migros operates food factories and numerous service firms, and is active even in ocean shipping. Its motto: *"social capital."*

Sources: Peter Höltschi and Alberto Venzago, "Migros, Marta, Mövenpick," *GEO Special Schweiz*, November 11, 1987, pp. 104–14; and Dominik Landwehr, personal communication, November 21, 1996.

RECENT TRANSFORMATIONS:
COMPETITIVE, AND LESS EMPLOYED

Specialize, Specialize!

The description of the character of the Swiss economy has so far remained static. It does not reflect the fact that during the course of this century most industries, in particular, the manufacturing and services have undergone deep changes in relation to their markets. This section gives a dynamic view of some of the major forces that have produced the current economic position of Switzerland.

Traditionally, Swiss foreign trade had been intrabranch trade. That means, for example, that Switzerland would export pharmaceuticals and would also produce most of the pharmaceuticals consumed in the country. It would import coal needed to power factories but would not have any coal to export. Exports were thus led by classical export industries. Imports had a similar degree of concentration in other branches. And yet other branches used to work for the internal market almost exclusively. After World War II, the pattern of industrial trade changed. Tariff barriers were lowered selectively, and in certain branches such as textiles, the domestic sector was invaded by competing importers. To counter the weight of the European Community (now, European Union), several small countries, among them Switzerland, founded the European Free Trade Association, and in 1972 Switzerland also concluded an association treaty with the European Community. Switzerland and its international partners engaged in more intrabranch trade; that is, goods of the same sector would

Modern Switzerland: The head of the design department at ASCOM, a leading Swiss telecommunications company, prepares for his weekly staff meeting. Photographer, Matthias Wehrlin.

be imported as well as exported. For example, machines accounted for 27 percent of the Swiss exports in 1994, but also for 21 percent of all imports. The primary effect of intrabranch trade was that it increased the pressure on businesses to specialize. Instead of offering goods and services in a wide range of typical branch activities, firms would concentrate on small segments that gave them a leadership role. For example, one of the leading Swiss paper factories moved out of newsprint paper for the local market, with its low margins, and into high-quality, special-purpose copying papers serving a worldwide clientele. Locational factors of the entire country grew relatively less important for the international division of labor; instead, competitive advantages of specific firms acquired a greater relative weight. This planted the seed for the later transfer of production capacity and increasingly also research and development of major exporting firms to other countries while the domestic sector hung on to its protective clutches wherever it could.

The sociological significance of specialization lies in its multidimensional effects: economic, cultural, and political. Managers and professionals of Swiss firms with wide international activities immerse in the whirlpool of global change and competition that the rest of the nation does not personally meet, or only in a mild version as tourists and media consumers. The domestic sector strives hard to follow technologically; culturally, it stays at home. The changing pattern of comparative advantages, in firms as well as in the workforce, teamed up with the federalist system to give rise to the new traditionalist—cosmopolitan polarity apart from the old left–right dimension.

At the same time, Switzerland offered foreign firms an attractive institutional framework. Since the fifties many have established their administrative centers in Switzerland. Political stability, a stable currency in relation to the US dollar and the British pound sterling, favorable foreign exchange and tax conditions, privileges for holding companies, central location in Europe, good communications and the high quality and motivation of the labor force were leading factors. In these foreign-dominated centers as many employees are working nowadays as in the domestic financial institutions (Bernegger 1992: 64–65).

Full Employment Is Gone

The years 1950 through 1973 were, as in many other industrial countries, years of strong, almost uninterrupted, economic growth, causing real per capita incomes to double. Labor markets were completely dried out; foreign workers were admitted in large numbers, taking over many of the manual jobs and helping the Swiss to unprecedented upward mobility. The fiscal position was strong; the state was able to expand the breadth and depth of its activity in response to the problems of modernization and the complexity of society. Within 15 years, the government quota nearly doubled, from 20 percent in 1960 to 35 percent in 1976.

The oil price shock of 1973 interrupted worldwide growth. Starting from 1975, the Swiss had to deal with the phenomenon of unemployment. At first unemployment was mild, mitigated by the departure of foreign workers, who were often the first to lose jobs. Otherwise, scant note was taken of the changing economic climate in the world. Switzerland did not reduce the protection of its domestically oriented sectors, and its long-term adaptation problems did not receive serious public debate. Economic health seemed excellent; Switzerland continued to surpass most other countries in savings and investment rates. But beneath the surface, things changed. The dynamic export sector continued its transformation. Initially, it was production capacity that was moved to low-wage countries while company headquarters in Switzerland would typically retain service centers for research and development, administration, planning, and marketing; in recent years, however, R&D investment abroad has surpassed new capacity at home. The economy started limping; growth was consistently slower in the late seventies and eighties, and Switzerland got trapped at the low end of labor productivity growth among industrial nations during that period.

Structural changes were accelerated. In a span of 10 years only, traditional industries shrank considerably while new branches grew almost explosively. For example, employment in textile production shrank by 30 percent between 1986 and 1994. During the same period, however, education added a strong 42 percent. Of great concern was the fact that chemicals and pharmaceuticals, the prime success branch in the Swiss economy, only saw modest employment gains (+7 percent), a reflection of its overseas capacities growing faster. In general, classical manufacturing branches are giving way to the expanding services (for example, education) or to whole-system solutions of mixed manufacturing-service character (for example, environmental protection). Competition for manufacturing locations became stiffer with the end of the Cold War when several Eastern European countries with their relatively well-trained workforce and low wages became accessible for Western investors. A case that attained public fame in Switzerland concerned Calida, a maker of up-market pajamas and underwear. Their wares had a reputation for durability, and a popular joke had it that Swiss husbands wore the same pair of Calida pajamas from bridal night to burial. In 1983, when Hungary was spearheading economic reforms in the socialist bloc, Calida moved certain sewing operations there. In 1990, a year after the fall of the Berlin Wall signified the end of the Cold War, Calida built an entire new factory in Hungary, where wage costs are 5 to 10 times lower than in Switzerland. While initially only a few hundred jobs were migrated, the loss of a proud manufacturing icon was painfully noted by the Swiss at large.

It was not to be the last defection of well-known enterprises. In 1992, the Swiss people rejected the government's bid to join the European Economic Area, which also would have exposed the domestically oriented sector to greater competition. The self-imposed isolation has further lessened comparative advantages for Swiss industry while it may

TABLE 20

Unemployment Rates in Various Countries

Country	1997 Rate
France	12.5%
Germany	11.8
Sweden	6.5
Great Britain	5.2
Switzerland	*4.9*
United States	4.6
Japan	3.5

Note: Date are for October for some countries and November for others.

Source: "Economic Indicators," *The Economist,* December 13, 1997, p. 96.

have improved them for banking and insurance (the Swiss currency, affected by the risks of European monetary unification, is favored by foreign investors; its high value then penalizes exporters).

With its adaptation problems growing, unemployment has reached higher levels in subsequent recessions. In 1994, 3.8 percent of the workforce were officially called unemployed, but hidden unemployment through early retirement and voluntary withdrawal, particularly among women and foreigners, may be considerable. Since then, the Swiss unemployment rate has increased somewhat more (to 4.9 percent by late 1997, exceeding the US rate!), but the important point is that it has remained way below those of its neighbors, countries that are members of the European Union, particularly Germany (see Table 20). Unemployment basically hits the working population; business may have more optimistic opinions. And, indeed, it recently reconfirmed Switzerland as one of the world leaders in competitiveness (Rodger 1996: IV). Perspectives are thus becoming divided: Switzerland is losing its privileged status as social *and* economic miracle country while it remains an economic power to be counted.

SECTORAL VIEWS: THE GROWTH OF SERVICES

Readers familiar with the long-term changes of economic sectors in other advanced countries will by now have recognized a familiar image. Switzerland also has followed the well-known pattern of the long-term decline of agriculture, forestry, and mining (the so-called primary sector), and of the growth of manufacturing (the secondary sector) until it shrank under the expansion of the services industry (the tertiary sector). Thus, had one in every five employed persons in 1950 still been a farmer, agriculture's share in total employment came down to a puny 5.5 percent by 1991. Manufacturing peaked—speaking of its relative employment share—in the sixties (46 percent). Its share in 1991, 34 percent, was still robust, indicative of the important industrial base. Services overtook manufacturing in the seventies. This change of predominance (a process sometimes called *tertiarization*) happened more than 20 years later than in the United States. Even today, though it provided two-thirds of all jobs in 1994, the Swiss tertiary sector is some 10 percentage points weaker than in the United States.

Sectoral changes are sociologically important because they are related to the growth of social inequality. A gross measure is provided by differences in the value added per employee. This index varies more widely within the service industries than within manufacturing and construction. Take these two extreme examples: Banking and insurance, with 5.4 percent of the employment, claimed 11.3 percent of the national value creation in 1992. The hospitality industry, with a similar number of employees, contributed only 3.2 percent. Within manufacturing, the chemical and energy branches created value per employee well above the average, but the low-performing branches did not lag that far behind. What happens is that with the tertiarization of the economy, some branches pay their professionals very high salaries and benefits while at the same time poor jobs are created in other service industries. This source of growing income inequality is well known from the United States; in Switzerland, poor jobs may not be as close to the poverty line, but the direction is the same. In the following pages, the three sectors will be briefly surveyed for their political, social structural, and cultural relevance.

Agriculture: Expensive Guardian of the Environment

Swiss agriculture relies on small farms with an average of 20 hectares land, a third smaller than the European Union mean. In 1990, 240,000 persons were employed on 90,000 farms, most of them owner–family members. Due to natural conditions—hilly and mountainous country—about three-quarters of the agricultural incomes is from meat, milk, and cheese. Switzerland is not self-sufficient in food grain and produce. Productivity has grown strongly despite very far-reaching protection policies; a third of all farmers active in 1940 are nowadays producing almost double the output. Generous subsidies have helped; the government calculates them on the principle of wage parity with the manufacturing sector. The Swiss farm subsidy quota is the highest in the world; it has grown considerably over the last 15 years. The Swiss taxpayer, as Table 21 shows, maintains the price of farm products at almost double the world market price. Thus, in 1995, the farmers of tiny Switzerland received $6.1 billion in subsidies, almost a third of what the

TABLE 21

Agricultural Subsidies

Country	Producer Subsidy Equivalents
Switzerland	81%
Japan	78
Europe	48
United States	15
Australia	10

Data and sources: EU (1987/88) Beat Hotz-Hart, Stefan Maeder, and Patrick Vock, *Volkswirtschaft der Schweiz* (Zurich: vdf Hochschulverlag AG an der ETH Zurich, 1995), p. 178; others (1995) "Farming," *The Economist,* June 1, 1996, p. 101.

United States plowed into its mammoth farm sector. In no other private industry are jobs defended with such public largesse, and the fierce resistance of the Swiss farmers to the European Economic Area is easy to understand. Many farmers are still living in tight circumstances, off small mountain farms sustained with 15 or 20 cows at most. Income support is being justified also with the service that these farmers render for the preservation of a healthy environment and of a beautiful countryside, a boon for the public and especially for the tourism industry. Forests, an essential part of Switzerland's beauty (30 percent of the land is under trees), are in part owned by farmers. Forest management is tightly regulated, with strict replanting rules; subsidies to forest owners are seen to be defending the environment and the cultural heritage. More than in any other sector of the private economy, the Swiss are prepared to acknowledge the noneconomic functions of agriculture and forestry and to pay for them.

The subsidies do distort the market; they create surpluses that cost the taxpayer dearly. However, they are seen as a holding operation, keeping farmers on the land who otherwise would be difficult to absorb in productive jobs elsewhere. This is slowing down the concentration process in Swiss agriculture, but it will not stop it.

Manufacturing: Let Me Use Your Technology First

Chemicals, machines, watches, electric and electronic goods, and high-value textiles are important industrial branches, but by no way the only ones. The manufacturing base is broad and diversified. That does not mean that the Swiss industry makes everything; we have already used the word *specialization* ad nauseam to characterize the industrial strategy of this small country. It supplies selective market segments with specialties, with highly differentiated product palettes in each of them. A list of strong and weak points of Swiss industry would probably include

1. Precision and quality, punctual delivery, and good service.
2. No mass producing big industries—small and medium-sized firms dominate.
3. Orientation toward technology and product, and to a lesser degree toward the market or alternative investment.
4. Deep manufacturing and low outsourcing of processes.
5. Expensive, highly qualified, and motivated workforce.
6. Beneficial neighborhood with financial institutions and conservative finance structure.
7. More regional decentralization in manufacturing than in other countries.

(Holz-Hart, Maeder, and Vock 1995: 182 and passim).

Several branches have disappeared, are endangered, or have changed character completely over time. For example, Switzerland has stopped making automobiles, but it is engaged in research in electric automobiles. The impact of globalization is particularly well illustrated by the fate of the textile industry: Under the onslaught of low-wage countries, Swiss mills are closing by the dozens. But narrow segments are being held. If you want to wrap your bride in the world's most exquisite lace, it will probably be Swiss. Textiles, in fact, illustrate the transition particularly well: From fabric and clothes, manufacturing moved on to textile machines. In 1986, Switzerland produced 13 percent of the world's textile machines. In certain segments, market shares were much higher, 45 percent for weaving looms, and 100 percent for special devices preparing loom work. This market honors qualities that are close to Swiss core values: precision, reliability, and service organized for continuous, heavy operation. The rapport between the Swiss suppliers and foreign customers is close and long-standing. Price is a secondary consideration.

The internationalization of the most successful Swiss manufacturing industries is progressing fast, and one wonders when they will cease to be essentially Swiss. Chemicals and pharmaceuticals are a case in point. The industry grew on a very successful strategy to market specialties worldwide, doubling the number of its jobs in Switzerland between 1946 and 1990. But the international composition of the firms changed at the same time, hardly noticed by the Swiss public during the years of growth. Cost considerations, the high regulatory density in Switzerland, and marketing strategies privileged new production capacities in other countries. More recently, management, research, and development functions are being decentralized. Large companies have created hundreds, sometimes thousands, of autonomous profit centers worldwide, of which only a minority remain based in Switzerland. Many firms go global also in their capital markets. Poorly informed people still treasure the illusion of mighty Swiss companies while actual ownership may already be foreign.

For the manufacturing that still takes place on Swiss soil, the strategic options are dictated by size, factor endowment, and tradition. As we said earlier, Switzerland does not have the means to lead new strategic technologies such as computers. Rather, it relies strongly on innovation in specialized niches. When new technologies reach the market, Swiss industry mixes them with its product-specific traditional competencies. It buys technology rather than developing it, in order to take "first user" applications to the world market.

Services: The Gnomes' Leadership

Switzerland is in the middle field of other advanced countries as regards the importance of the tertiary sector. The composition of the Swiss service industries differs notably from that of other countries. Banking and insurance hold a very strong position. Three of the big Swiss banks are major international banks. Smaller banks primarily tend to a domestic clientele. Not all commercial banks are private; the cantons operate banks with government guarantees for savings. The banking sector is likely to see strong rationalization in the years to come, shedding thousands of jobs. (As this book goes to press, two of the three giants have just merged, creating the world's second-biggest bank.) Other important branches are tourism and social services, which include health care.

One of the major questions that the Swiss must ask about their growing service sector concerns its independence from manufacturing. While it is well acknowledged that manufacturing and construction benefit from close relations with Swiss financial institutions, the comparative advantages that service firms draw from this neighborhood are less appreciated. Internationally, Swiss service providers make money not least from expertise they acquired in business with the Swiss manufacturing sector. For engineering, that is obvious. It also applies to other service branches. For example, the growing tendency to rely on whole-system providers makes direct cooperation with diverse Swiss manufacturing branches an asset for financial and technical consultancy businesses; if they lack experience in the manufacturing world, foreign customers may find the Swiss service sector expertise too narrow. Deindustrialization—the continuous transfer of manufacturing capacity to other countries—or extremely specialized manufacturing could then backfire on the service sector. Switzerland's problem is to keep the right mix of manufacturing and services while acknowledging that it can excel only in a small number of technological and service clusters.

TECHNOLOGICAL POSITION: BETTER OLD AND WISE THAN YOUNG AND SMART

If cheap capital has financed a technologically advanced manufacturing base, it is the quality of the Swiss workforce that puts it to good use. As was shown in the section on education, the Swiss professional education system essentially sends students on two different avenues. A large number of youth complete two- to four-year vocational apprenticeships, with time shared between office or factory floor and government-run trade schools. The apprenticeship system has supplied Switzerland with a steady flow of workers who are qualified at an intermediate level and are disciplined, practical, and competent in their trades. The technical universities, run by the government, are world class, and there are a number of intermediate technical schools, that are also well reputed. But their output is too small for the needs of the Swiss economy. The chemical and pharmaceutical industry, for example, is relying on expatriates for almost half of its research and development positions.

In an education system that shares responsibility between private industry and government, the government's position is strong. When it comes to the actual research and development, business takes the lead. About three-quarters of the R&D effort is financed by business, and the government's involvement has remained low and chiefly in basic research. Swiss researchers have been effective in a number of fields; that is, their findings are appreciated by the international scientific community. Above-average use of Swiss research results is being made in the fields of biology, mathematics, earth and space sciences, engineering, biomedical research, chemicals and pharmaceuticals, and physics. There are counterexamples, too. The Swiss scientific community has shown activism also in clinical medicine, but this has had little international effect. One wonders if it is the close interaction with Swiss patients that removes medical researchers from the English-speaking international research community, or the small size of the domestic market that slows the pace of innovation.

The point is that the list gets much shorter when we look at the fields with heavy private research and development. Again the law of specialization prevails. Only three fields—chemicals and pharmaceuticals, electric and electronic goods, and machinery and metalworking—account between them for 82 percent of the Swiss R&D expenditure. In the private sector, basic research is done only in chemicals and pharmaceuticals; other branches are content to adapt external results. Therefore, only one sector can claim to be doing leading-edge technology research. With limited resources, concentration of the R&D effort on a small number of fields has sustained competitive innovation. By the number of patents filed, Switzerland is among the 10 most inventive nations. When we consider patent activity relative to its small population, it outranks even Japan and Germany.

But patenting is very uneven across fields. The Swiss specialize along conservative lines. Old fields are hardly ever abandoned, new ones rarely conquered. For example, Switzerland registers relatively few patents in biotechnology, one of the fastest-expanding technologies. Watchmaking and textile machines are at the peak of the Swiss patenting activity; worldwide, however, these branches are barely holding or even decreasing the speed of their innovations. As a result, the share of high-technology goods in the Swiss exports portfolio has very slowly decreased from 45 percent to 40 percent over the past 25 years. That is in contrast to other advanced industrial countries like Japan and the United States, who were able to upgrade their high-technology shares by 10 percentage points.

All considered, the picture of the Swiss economy is marked by clusters of strength side by side with areas that are almost totally blank. An eclectic list of strong areas would include banking, insurance, pharmaceuticals, base material chemistry, process technology, industrial control, and tool-making machines. Telecommunication and computers, optics, and automobiles provide contrast by their absence or weakness. The Swiss economy is a mature one; it builds on old strengths, and lives off them. Only now are the Swiss waking up to the fact that they have not done enough to stimulate innovation. In sharp contrast to the financial institutions of the United States, there are hardly any venture capitalists in Switzerland. Swiss banks have for a long time preferred to loan to well-established businesses (and are remarkably willing to help them through difficult times), at the disadvantage of young entrepreneurs who try to obtain finance for new business ideas. Several cantonal administrations, technical universities, and banks are now grappling with new kinds of institutional arrangements, such as technoparks, to support business upstarts and relocations, but these are as yet small beginnings toward more aggressive industrial changes.

CONCLUSION

We have learned that the Swiss economy has highly performing sectors for a range of goods and services much larger than chocolates, cheese, and watches that make up the traditional image. Pharmaceuticals and chemicals are the prime example of such a leading sector in manufacturing while banks and insurance epitomize the strong service industries. But due to the obligation of a small country to specialize, there are also important sectors from which the Swiss are practically absent, such as the manufacture of computers and automobiles. The Swiss economy is tightly connected with foreign economies, particularly by the high density of multinational companies that are headquartered in Switzerland. This strong outward orientation is very different from that of Swiss politics, which basically is inward-looking. Switzerland's adaptation to a changing outside world is led by the technologically advanced sector of the economy, which is more innovative than the polity.

At the same time, a large part of the economy, primarily businesses that produce for the domestic market and labor, have always depended on politically sanctioned protection from competition. Through business associations and trade unions, as described in the chapter on politics, these economic agents form a tight network with local and federal administrations. Such a system has consequences that go way beyond the economy to fashion social structure. In the Swiss case, two outcomes have to be noted: The regulated economy helped to strengthen the middle class and, side by side with industries competing in the world market, has deepened the rift between cosmopolitans and traditionalists.

The international competitiveness of the Swiss economy is considered good, although possibly declining. With its political isolation from the European Union, high cost levels, and lack of participation in new pioneering industries, the old strengths may slowly wear out. The Swiss may then lose their privileged position and, while probably remaining a medium-sized economic power for a long while, have to settle for a more modest seat in the concert of prosperous nations.

FURTHER READING

Hotz-Hart, Beat; Stefan Maeder; and Patrick Vock. *Volkswirtschaft der Schweiz.* Zurich: vdf Hochschulverlag AG an der ETH Zurich, 1995. A very comprehensive portrait of the Swiss economy.

Social Problems

"Mrs. Meyer always manages to dress her three sons tidily" is a comment that still rings in my ears from childhood days. It was directed, patronizingly, at one of the very few families that at the time were definitely classified as poor. The Meyers (name changed), who lived in a decommissioned school extension building, "unwisely" had several children with disabilities and had to be looked after by the commune. Poverty in post-war Switzerland was an increasingly rare phenomenon and was sometimes moralized as personal failure; whereas for other groups like small farmers in the mountains, it was idealized as part of a hardy survival spirit. But by and large it was simply abolished by the social security and welfare systems that were put in place under the pressure of an effective socialist movement.

The reappearance of poverty over the past two decades has therefore come as a shock to many Swiss. In this chapter, it is used to exemplify the kinds of social problems that tend to disturb the sleep of a prosperous society. Other problems that have keenly alarmed the Swiss include drug addiction and the numbers and integration problems of immigrants. This list is by far not exhaustive of social problems in Switzerland, but the ways the Swiss have been dealing with those three illustrate both social change and collective learning.

"PROBLEMS" MISSING IN THE VOCABULARY

In the American social studies literature, books with the term "social problems" in their title abound. In Switzerland, they must be rare. Using those key words, a search for German-language books in current supply returned zero; another, tapping into a Swiss newspaper database, produced articles coded under "poverty," "social security," and "social welfare." The fact is that the Swiss, including their sociologists, hardly use the generic term "social problems." All will agree that social problems do exist in Switzerland; examples of problem areas frequently evoked are

TABLE 22

Evolution of Social Insurance

Major Programs by Hazard	Year First Implemented
Military service	1902
Sickness and accidents	1913
Old age, widows and orphans: Government assistance	1948
Unemployment	1952
Children: Mandatory wage support for employed parents	1953
Disability	1960
Old age: Mandatory employers' pension schemes	1985
Old age; Tax-advantages savings schemes	1987

Source: Simplified from Peter Füglistaler-Wasmer, *Sozialpolitische Massnahmen im Kampf gegen die Armut in der Schweiz* (Berne, Stuttgart, Wien: P. Haupt Verlag, 1992), p. 82.

AIDS, drugs, and the new poverty. But these and others are not placed together in one broad category. They are treated separately.

The reasons for the absence of a generic, all-encompassing term must remain speculative. A somewhat cynical suspicion would be that the large and prosperous middle class does not perceive a sizable difference between the ideals of Swiss society and its actual achievements. But that would deny a large majority the capacity for compassion and insight. A more plausible hypothesis is that the Swiss prefer to debate what they see as solutions already in place, but increasingly eroded by fiscal woes, the aging of the population, and political indecision. Public debate (and also the book titles searched) rings with terms like "Swiss social state," "social policies," "social insurance," "assistance," and, again and again, "social security." The latter also includes welfare programs. The defense of these systems, incrementally legislated and put into effect over more than a 100 years (see Table 22), mobilizes public opinion and political energies. While there are doubts about the long-term financial viability of major elements of social security, there is nothing like a broad, ideologically concerted attack on "social welfare as we know it." The consensus that welfare payments for those who need them must not be limited in time seems to hold.

Rather, it is the principle on which social security and welfare systems are built that obstructs a generic social problems view. Assistance is activated by well-defined hazards such as old age or unemployment, regardless of the objective needs of the individual. Most branches of social security are guided by causality, not finality (Füglistaler-Wasmer 1992: 82). This mode of operation leaves a considerable residual risk out of public focus. It includes such diverse groups as the chronically unemployed, drug addicts, convicts, and, to some degree, foreigners. They still qualify for minimal welfare for as long as they need it as well as for some specific programs. They therefore do not turn into intractable social problems, but they do not usually receive the kinds of concern that are reserved for large interest groups.

In the following, the situation of three problem groups is analyzed: the poor, foreigners, and drug addicts.

THE ELEVATOR GOES TO THE BASEMENT: THE POOR

A Third of the US Poverty Rate?

Poverty became a national issue in the United States in the 60s. A generation later, in the second half of the 80s, Switzerland followed suit. This delay was not an instance of an international issue that the Swiss, in their conservativism, reacted to belatedly (as they did with regard to many other social and cultural changes in the Western world), but it had simple domestic reasons: The country, relative to its population size, had few people who were poor. If for anything, their culture and politics would have predisposed the Swiss for an intense public debate. The ubiquitous tendency to favor the middle ground in most questions of life and society, the strength of the organized left parties, and the expanding welfare state would not have tolerated large-scale poverty. Thus, when the first studies into poverty were published around 1980, looking specifically at the situation of retirees, they caused only faint echoes. The situation was not considered alarming. That changed a few years later when the consequences of global transformations started to make themselves felt. But as late as 1990, poverty researchers felt obliged to ask in the title of their study: "Do we have any poor?" (Hainard et al. 1990). The discipline in Switzerland is young and poorly coordinated. Most of the studies are confined to a canton or major city; their definitions of poverty vary, and only a few relate financial data, primarily from tax records, to life-situation variables. Moreover, the poverty line is fixed some way above the level of income at which the poor can no longer afford the basic necessities of life. When measuring poverty, the official terminology does not speak of the poor, but of "households in precarious income situations." Some studies take the guaranteed old-age minimum income as a breakpoint, which in 1987 was about $1,000 per month for a single-person household. Others use the 50 percent level of the average household income in their cantons. Most of the studies are one-point shots; time series do not exist. The state of knowledge on poverty is therefore gravely underdeveloped compared to the US situation.

Not surprisingly, the multitude of definitions has produced an absurd amount of variation in poverty estimates. The range of persons living in "precarious income situations" in various cantons and at various points in time between 1976 and 1987 went from 4.7 percent to 14.7 percent (Füglistaler-Wasmer 1992: 58). Some systematic data modeling was done in the canton of St. Gallen offering a larger number of income breakpoints and corresponding estimates of group size. For example, in

1987, 5.2 percent of the inhabitants had incomes below the ones guaranteed under old-age social security, and 14.7 percent lived on less than 50 percent of the average income (Füglistaler-Wasmer 1992: 69). Comparisons with US poverty definitions are difficult because of differences in household income equivalency scales, in purchasing power, and in the value of public goods such as transport. In the United States, a nonfarm family of four was considered poor in 1993 when their income fell below $14,763. By that definition, 15.5 percent of all Americans were poor. Using the US Bureau of Labor equivalency scale, and adjusting for various factors, I estimated 3 to 5 percent of people in St. Gallen to have been in a similarly bad situation. The federal government put this figure higher in February 1996 when it ventured a global estimate of 500,000 persons living in precarious income situations. This amounts to 7.1 percent of the population. The public welfare roll at the same time comprised 265,000 persons assisted (Lassueur and Pirolt 1996), or 3.8 percent of the population. As the welfare system is commonly credited as being fairly responsive, a sensible poverty estimate would be found somewhere in the middle between the easy-to-figure 3.8 percent assisted and the still somewhat arbitrary 7.1 percent launched by Federal Councilors. This would place the Swiss poverty rate at about one-third of the US value. A 5 percent rate would also be close to that of most other central European countries (Kerbo 1996: 248).

Single-Parent Families at Highest Risk

While we do not have a definitive answer as to the prevalence of poverty in Switzerland, its associated social conditions are known with better precision. Some of the poverty hazards are strikingly similar to American conditions; others offer surprises. Table 23, based on the St. Gallen study, displays the relative risk for being poor depending on social status.

Several findings spring to the eye. Despite well-developed social insurance for the elderly and those with disabilities, members of these groups are disproportionately more often poor. The working poor are few; unskilled workers are twice as likely to be poor as those with more education, but they still face lower-than-average poverty hazards. Marriage is a safeguard against poverty. Having children does not expose married couples to greater risks of poverty. It may seem a surprise that foreigners were not at greater risk than the natives, but this effect is artificial; using short-term work and stay permits, Switzerland exports many of those among its foreign population who are most likely to become poor. By 1996, anyway, about half of those on the public welfare roll were foreigners, indicating that their countrywide indigent rate was higher.

The greatest poverty hazard is reserved for single-parent families. Four-fifths of these parents are women. Switzerland thus shares in the feminization of poverty that marks the recent evolution of social problems in many advanced countries. Definition problems make it difficult to

TABLE 23

Social Factors Associated with Poverty

Status	Relative Poverty Risk
Employed	−39%
Retirees	+73
Persons with disabilities	+121
Married couples, no children, before retirement	−74
Married couples with children, before retirement	−73
Parents paying alimony or child support	−64
Single-parent households	+182
Foreigners	−6
Swiss citizens	+2
Skilled workers	−70
Lower employees	−68
Unskilled workers	−30

Note: Equivalence income limit: CHF 12,000.

Source: Calculated after Peter Füglistaler-Wasmer, *Sozialpolitische Massnahmen im Kaupf gegen der Schweiz* (Berne, Stuttgart, Wien: P. Haupt Verlag, 1992), p. 73.

directly compare the 18.6 percent poverty rate among single-parent families in St. Gallen with the 43 percent found for single white mothers with children under 18 in the United States (Schaefer and Lamm 1989: 232; the rates are 67 percent for Hispanics and 68 percent for blacks), but in both countries the poverty hazard for this group is several times that of the average population. As studies from other nations confirm, this phenomenon has become universal regardless of welfare legislation. The causes of more numerous poor, single-parent families may not simply lie in the more frequent break-up of families. In the United States, the dramatic increase in single-mother households has been faulted. But in Switzerland, the share of lone-parent families in the total of all families with children has not dramatically changed. It was 11.6 percent in 1960 and 13.6 percent in 1990 (the corresponding figure for the United States in 1984 was 26.0 percent). During that period, the percentage of divorced persons almost tripled. Obviously, family breakdown is not a leading cause, even though some complain that Swiss women are just one husband away from poverty. Suter and others (1996) showed that female-headed families in Zurich, while they were in precarious income situations, were more likely to suffer multiple deficiencies than such family heads whose incomes were sufficient. The poorer group had twice as many mothers with only mandatory schooling, were twice as often unemployed, had weaker social networks to support them, and had more traumatic biographies. But the same study showed that these families moved out of poverty at an astonishing speed. Within one year, one-third had worked their way above the poverty line (Suter et al. 1996: 46). The authors attributed the unexpectedly mild predicament of the group to an effective public welfare system and to the level of child support that fathers paid. This is not to say that many of those women would move up to the middle class, but their impoverishment was halted.

Just as much as for the national incidence of poverty, the lack of longitudinal studies limits our findings on the extent to which the Swiss move in and out of poverty. The character of poverty itself is changing. One of the next groups headed for greater poverty risks is the long-term unemployed, but we do not yet know much about their situation. The current evidence points to poverty rates that are substantially lower than the American sort, adding belief to the thesis of a country consolidated in a broad middle class. Most of the elevator trips are between floors 3 and 6, and with few people taken to the basement or the top floor.

THE OTHER SWITZERLAND: FOREIGNERS

One in Five

No account of the Swiss social structure can sidestep the importance of the foreign population. The term *foreigners* is commonly used for those to whom Americans refer as aliens or immigrants. Almost one in every five residents in Switzerland is a foreigner. The 18.1 percent who responded as foreigners in the 1990 census is almost four times higher than the average rate of 4.7 percent for foreigners living in the European Union countries (Levy et al. 1997: Ch. 4, p. 38). The Swiss situation in this regard is exceptional.

In the fifties and sixties, foreign workers arrived in large numbers because Swiss wages were growing below total productivity, and it made sense for businesses to use labor-intensive technologies. Immigration became a public issue in the sixties, and several initiatives to curb it were so close to success in the ballots that they prompted the government to impose greater limitations. We have already dealt with the massive influx into menial jobs and its effects on the social mobility of the Swiss. A much smaller group of foreigners consists of the expatriates working in international organizations, such as the United Nations in Geneva, in the Swiss subsidiaries of foreign corporations, and as specialists in research and development–intensive branches of Swiss enterprises. Thus, the foreigners' share in R&D divisions in chemical concerns is as high as 40 percent, a result of the slow expansion of the Swiss tertiary education system not keeping pace with industry needs.

Problems with foreigners before 1980 were aptly summarized in a famous phrase of Swiss writer Max Frisch: "We called workers, and there came human beings." In the sixties the large majority of all foreigners were active workers, many with temporary status only. There were few elderly, children, and nonworking family members among them; Swiss immigration law at the time made family unifications very difficult. In the late eighties and nineties, the character of immigration and of the settled foreigners changed. In addition to workers actively recruited, a growing stream of uncalled and unwanted foreigners made their way into the country. Asylum seekers from countries in war and economic migrants from the Third World changed the composition of the foreign population and public perceptions. **Xenophobic** reactions became more common, and in 1990, the public was shocked to learn that the population had grown faster than anticipated, and that a large part of the increase was attributed to immigration and immigrants' fertility. A smaller portion of the foreigners were now working than 30 years back, while more of the Swiss had moved into employment. The fact that in the previous decades Swiss society had become more homogeneous at a middle-class level started to hamper the integration of foreigners. These were an underclass in a double bind: They either worked, and then, with growing unemployment, took away jobs from the Swiss, or they didn't work and strained public welfare budgets.

Recent Arrivals Were from Countries Farther Away

All that added to the radical change in the ethnic and cultural make-up. In the early stage, until about 1980, the integration of a large number of foreigners in Switzerland was facilitated by the fact that most of them were native of surrounding countries. The specificity of the immigration to Switzerland was easily understood: It was a small country that needed workers and obtained them from European Union countries with which it shared languages and culture, but it did not want to, or have to, join the Union politically. Later, cultural commonality with the immigrant population decreased; at the same time, the Swiss people became deeply divided over the possible integration with the European Union and its putative consequences for immigration and loss of national character. Table 24 shows the shrinking percentage of foreigners who are nationals of neighboring countries, and the growing share of those who arrived from outside Europe.

TABLE 24

Origin of Foreigners

	1960	1990
Surrounding countries	87.3%	44.5%
Other European countries	7.1	39.1
Other countries	5.6	16.4

Source: Werner Haug, *Vom Einwanderungsland zur Multikulturellen Migrationspolitik. Grundlagen fuer eine Schweizerische Migrationspolitik* (Berne: Federal Office of Statistics, 1995), p. 31.

CHAPTER 6

Examples of the communities falling into each of these categories are Italians (383,312 in 1990), former Yugoslavians (171,695), and Turks (81,210).

The presence of a large number of cultural strangers poses challenges to productive living together. Communication in offices and on the factory floor is more difficult. Schools struggle to accommodate more children who speak the language of instruction incompletely. In the *Volksschulen* of the urban cantons of Geneva and Basle, 40 percent of the students are foreigners; in some neighborhoods this rate exceeds 70 percent. Many of them fail in the academic track of the Swiss education system. Some of the newer immigrants hold very conservative notions of the place of women in family and society, manifest in the fact that 60 percent of all marriages between foreign men and Swiss women fail, mostly over cultural conflicts, as against 30 percent of all other sex and nationality combination marriages. Much note is taken of the foreigners' disproportionately high share in criminal convictions (44 percent in 1994), and some groups—former Yugoslavians and Albanians—are popularly reputed to be violent. Seldom is it said publicly that foreigners are concentrated in the low ranks of society, and that the delinquency rate of low-class people is very similar for both Swiss and foreigners.

The danger of vicious circles of marginalization is obvious. It is fueled by political contradictions. A stagnant economy and ballot initiatives by the traditionalist parties have turned the government very restrictive on immigration. Toward the European Union, it has to offer greater freedom for the movement of labor as a counterpart to desired access to markets. The two can be reconciled only by reversing immigration and work permits of non-Union foreigners, such as Yugoslavs and Turks. In 1991, the federal government proposed a cultural–legal framework to accommodate its torn-asunder policies. Known as the "Three-Circle Model," it vowed to liberalize immigration for European Union citizens. Quotas were foreseen for a small number of highly qualified professionals from the United States, Japan, and Canada. From other countries, only top managers, specialists, and trainees would be admitted. The classification fits neatly into current ideologies of advanced capitalist countries, which see themselves beleaguered by the billions of Third-World poor, while at the same time they need foreign labor both at the lower chores and the high professional ends. If this policy is implemented, the situation of "third-circle" country immigrants and of their children born in Switzerland will become more precarious.

Successful Integration

In contrast to the pessimism that inspired recent policy debates, post-war Switzerland has a successful record of integrating foreigners. One of the causes may lie in Switzerland's own cultural heritage as a nation in which several languages are spoken with equal rights. Shared work experience on the factory floor in the sixties and seventies, notably with Italians, prepared many of the Swiss for greater diversity, even those who did not command a second national language themselves. Swiss voters in areas with higher percentages of foreigners are more open to accelerated naturalization than their fellow citizens in more pure Swiss districts. Schools have offered an increasing array of remedial measures for foreign children with learning problems. Higher employment has become more accessible with time spent in Switzerland. The percentage of unskilled workers decreased among both men and women the more their status in Switzerland improved. Men in the 25–34-year age bracket may serve as an illustration: Among temporary workers and asylum seekers, it is 54 percent; among one-year permit holders and residents, it has fallen to 36 percent; and the "second generation"—those born in Switzerland—count only 10 percent unskilled among their working members. In earnings and hierarchical position, foreign men have overtaken Swiss women (Haug 1995: 50, 59, 61). Despite greater cultural diversity, inequality based on citizenship has been reduced to levels lower than those for gender inequality.

With social inequality growing in general, inequalities within the foreign population in Switzerland may well be increasing, too. At the bottom, an overproportionate number of women, youth with poor education, illegals, and recent arrivals from beyond the European Union are found. Xenophobic movements are being fed by Swiss who are losers of modernization. Some local areas have reached degrees of ethnic diversity that make them small New Yorks. Go to the 28,000 people Aussersihl neighborhood in Zurich, where Lenin in exile used to preach the gospel of proletarian unity worldwide. The leader of the communist revolution did not foresee that three generations after him, 110 nationalities would share the few square miles of humanity around his historical podium.

A LEARNING SOCIETY: DRUGS AND DOCTRINES
An Open Wound

Hardly any public issue illustrates the interplay of Swiss culture with other aspects, domestic and worldwide, better than the drug problem. The example is so graphic because the drug problem has been surprisingly amenable to local inspection. Zurich, seat of many of Switzerland's discreet banking gnomes, has had much unwanted publicity over the past 10 years. Small, concentrated badlands of illegal drug use thrived under the eyes of the media, earning the city the reputation as one of Europe's drug capitals. The Swiss drug problem had its own fascination at the crossways of numerous other developments. At the Platzspitz behind the National Museum and, later, on the tracks of the Letten train station, hundreds of addicts would congregate. These *misérables* were wasted in a crucible of cultural change, political protest, expert debates, federalist politics, and international crime. How to deal with drug abuse became a touchstone for a learning society, and a place for much national soul-searching (Zanoni 1994; Sorg 1994). Not

Social movements: Women politicians at the "Future Bikes" show, an event of the transportation alternatives movement. The driver is also finance director for the municipality of Berne. Photographer, Matthias Wehrlin.

only the local extent, but also the perceived character and the international connections of the problem have changed a great deal, and a timeline therefore seems to be an appropriate form to represent its evolving nature.

As a social problem, the modern wave of drug abuse—that is, other than tobacco and alcohol—is about 30 years old. Until 1950, the Swiss pharmaceutical industry used to manufacture morphium, cocaine, and heroin legally. Almost 95 percent of a yearly output of several tons was exported. Domestic consumers obtained the substances legally, through medical prescriptions. They were few, discreet, often upper class, or physicians themselves. Their habit did not create a social problem either when production was discontinued in 1950, under American pressure, and some of the users doubtlessly switched to foreign suppliers. These did not actively recruit users in Switzerland; in fact, the seed of the modern problem is traced to a different group altogether. Cannabis products were first noticed among guests of a Rolling Stones concert in 1965 and were used increasingly by protesting youths. Most of the early users were the sons and daughters of Swiss upper-middle-class families, imitated some years later by people of more modest means, including a substantial group of second-generation immigrants. Traffic was almost exclusively in Swiss hands.

The reaction of the Swiss political elite was a product of their time. Brought up in the ideologically sanitized war years, the people who governed in the late sixties were confused by the association of youth protest, a challenge, however feeble, to their rule, and the liberating message of pot. In their determination to stamp out cannabis, they completely over-looked the gathering storm of heroin. The 1975 revision of the federal law on illegal substances made not only the traffic, but for the first time also the use, of cannabis a crime. This policy would in the years to come tie up scarce police and criminal justice resources. Heroin dealers made their first, successful, offensive, and already in 1976 Zurich developed an open drug scene filled with ragged, destitute, hard-core addicts. The criminalization of addicts hardened, with several years of running battles between police and addicts, who would reconstitute their markets in ever new public places. By 1982, Zurich was sore with the presence of an estimated 3,000 junkies. Medical and social aid structures grew in parallel. Opposing views between the groups providing survival assistance and the repressive agencies led to ideological polarization, which was echoed in national politics roughly along the left–right dimension. But at first, the repressive line prevailed. Pressure to recognize addicts as medical patients was ineffective, notably because the Swiss medical associations did not speak out against the criminalization of users. The mediatized typical addict of the early eighties was no longer a middle-class person, but a skid-row junkie to whom few physicians and nurses felt attracted.

AIDS Forces a Policy Change

Then the AIDS epidemic broke. Men used drug addicts as prostitutes. The specter of husbands infecting their unknowing wives after a visit to the Zurich drug milieu haunted the nation. In the space of a few years, moral condemnation of drug users gave way to a—not-so-unselfish—concern for their health and stabilization. In 1985, the medical associations demanded that control of the HIV and hepatitis epidemics be given priority over repression, and in 1986 Zurich removed the ban on distributing clean injection material. AIDS made the authorities seek the cooperation of the addicts.

The sudden toleration threw public policy into disarray. The flood of heroin addicts coming to liberal Zurich from other parts of Switzerland and from abroad sent street prices up; this attracted a large presence of mafia gangs from Lebanon, the former Yugoslavia, and, in recent years, West Africa. The drug milieu grew more violent. The police had their hands tied in the face of massive traffic of drugs and stolen goods while the tiers of the Swiss polity issued contradicting instructions. In the summer of 1994, the open presence of several hundred hard-core addicts in a decommissioned railroad station in Zurich created a kind of national emergency. The authorities eventually drove them back into surrounding neighborhoods, but intense media coverage led to public debate taking stronger note of other European policy models. Harm reduction policies, including maintenance programs for selected users to receive opiates under medical supervision, gained prominence. At the same time, the Swiss people remained divided over such doctrinal questions as to whether addiction can be healed completely, or whether cannabis is a gateway to hard drugs. Conservative forces launched political initiatives that, if successful, would revive more repressive strategies, but one of the best publicized at the national level was rejected by a clear majority of voters in 1997. Diversity among cantons is proving strong also in matters of drug policy. Ironically, one of the cantons preaching a hard line is a major wine growing area; politicians there, while tough on pot, are understandably soft on alcohol.

The drugs and AIDS epidemics provided mutual reinforcement to scale up public education campaigns. Drug-related deaths peaked in 1992, and addiction has since then "stabilized on a high level." In 1995, between 40,000 and 50,000 persons in Switzerland were using hard drugs; regular and occasional cannabis users were thought to be around 450,000 (Baschek 1995). The street value of the traded heroin and cocaine was estimated to total around $1.7 billion, with another $400 million sold in cannabis. The United States, according to a presidential report, counted 2.7 million hard-core cocaine and heroin users in 1993 (Clinton 1996). Their consumption cost an estimated $50 billion. Those figures allow some comparisons.

Internationalization of a Problem

Although definitions may vary between the two countries, drug abuse seems to be less prevalent in Switzerland than in the United States. About 7 in every 1,000 Swiss were using hard drugs in 1995, compared to 11 per 1,000 Americans. But the value of the illegal drugs per user works out to be significantly higher in Switzerland, with an estimated $34,000 per year (United States: $18,500). This will guarantee Switzerland the attention of numerous criminal organizations. For example, mafias in the former communist states of Eastern Europe are trying to use the industrial capacity of their countries in order to launch new synthetic drugs in Western Europe, including Switzerland. The drug problem is also inextricably linked with state breakdown in distant countries and the influx of refugees, some of whom engage in criminal traffic. And on the side of those mandated to do something about the problem, the experience of other countries is eagerly being studied. As with many other areas of cultural and social change, the drug problem in Switzerland has been internationalized. The Swiss have learned that they will have to live with a substantial problem for a long time, just as other countries do.

CONCLUSION

As may be typical of the semantics of a prosperous society, the Swiss approach their social problems less from the diagnostic side than in deference to treatments that they think are already in place and so far have worked quite well, in long-tested social security and welfare systems.

But everybody agrees that these systems will come under strain from fiscal stringency and demographic change, while the nature of the social problems keeps changing, or their severity increases. Considerable social learning is therefore required. Sometimes this is still at the diagnostic stage, such as in the case of the new poverty where the plurality of definitions in the federalist system has obscured the extent of the problem. Some radical learning took place under the onslaught of new problems. The AIDS epidemic obliged the medical, social work, and law enforcement professions to work out less repressive strategies to deal with drug addiction (politics had to follow suit grudgingly). And certain phenomena have been defined as social problems only recently when their environment had changed sufficiently to do so. Thus, foreigners have come to constitute a social problem, in a society that had made good progress in integrating unusually high numbers of them, particularly since the Swiss began seeing job opportunities dwindle for their own.

The common denominator of those social problems, and possibly of others too, is that they are increasingly becoming aligned with those of other countries. The poverty rate in Switzerland may be only a third of the American, but the feminization of poverty seems to be marching on inexorably in Switzerland just as elsewhere. Modern drug addiction, initially regarded as depravity of isolated addicts (by conservatives, or as bohemian charm by liberals), now involves organized international mafias that threaten much wider sectors of society. And, while one would expect foreign media consumption and international tourism would prepare the Swiss well for the challenges of multiculturalism, this is much less so when the immigrant communities are seen as increasingly numerous, culturally distant, and competing for a shrinking pie. This, too, is a perception that is shared by significant groups of natives in Switzerland and in all surrounding countries. Switzerland, it may be concluded, is less and less of a unique case also in the realm of social problems.

Outlook: Trains of Society

The west–east intercity express train leaves Geneva one minute to every hour, 16 times a day. It paves its way between the Lake and the United Nations into open country, greets the French Alps to its right, vineyards on the slopes of the Jura to the left. In Lausanne, passengers to Italy may transboard; the express swings up the grade into the Midlands. We leave the Protestantism of Calvin and the cosmopolitan feeling of the western corner; the countryside has a more earthen quality and, while still French-speaking, for a while is solidly Catholic territory. Shortly after Fribourg, shooting over the Saane River, we enter Alemannic Switzerland. One and three-quarters hours after the journey began, Berne, the capital, beckons her welcome. On the opposite platform waits a train to Germany to the north. Flying eastward, however, the express does not bother about the numerous industrial towns any more than about farms, orchards, and forests until it reaches Zurich, center of commerce and hub to distant continents. Zurich is hectic, but after the airport, the pace slows down by stops at lesser towns. The train gently climbs, comes in closer view of the Alps, though never near their feet. Four and a half hours into its journey, it ends in St. Gallen, with the German and Austrian shores glimmering from the far side of Lake Constance.

Sociologists could, of course, populate the train with members of the groups that frequent certain stations more than others. Thus, we would expect to find more federal employees traveling between, say, Berne and neighboring Fribourg than between Zurich and St. Gallen. And, during the month of October, farmers in traditional garb would congregate in St. Gallen, on their way to the national agricultural fair. Such insights would be legion, and most would be trivial. What this book has attempted to show is the massive contrasts in historic places, current status, and future prospects that the train lets us visit over the entire spread of a country within less than half a day. From the global debates at the United Nations to the cattle prizes of the fair, the train connection is largely metaphorical; the two sets of participants do not often intermingle. But for most other events, the connection is real, close, massive. Trains move many sorts of people, not only the expected ones to the expected places, but also those to be brought into conviviality from opposite and indifferent ends.

As with any powerful icon, the line between metaphor and physics, between ideal and grudging reality is thin. Swiss trains are parentheses that hold together an unlikely diversity of groups and cultures. The mixing stays incomplete; apart from the trains and the railway stations, the communities continue their own business, different lifestyles, and mutual ignorance. But thanks to the trains, peace, sweet commerce, friendly visits also abound.

Can this idyllic version of a small country go on? For prognostications using the train metaphor, we would need more solid traffic statistics. But it seems that pressures are mounting against the trains. The international jet set descending on Geneva may be growing faster than those who arrive by the east–west express. In Berne, a capital without a proper airport, more people may actually be using trains, but do as many of them travel beyond their dormitory towns and beyond Zurich's international airport? In Zurich, we are certain, those who no longer can afford intercity trips at discretion have become more numerous, and so have the ones who travel by car because it is more individualistic. And will the farmers around St. Gallen really care if fewer trains connect them with Geneva, or will they prefer more generous local bus services? If the fiscal crisis of the state obliges to reduce the number of trains, how many will be the minimum in order to hold the country together?

Said the trolley man who sold me the coffee: "You know, on the south trains I have the elderly, with their day excursions through the Gotthard tunnel and into the Italian sunshine. They sing, I sell a lot of wine. It's more slurs, but also more tips. But here, between Zurich and Berne, it's strictly business. Office suits. Lots of coffee, lots of croissants. No compliments, scant tips. You could think we were two different countries. But it's the same trains."

BIBLIOGRAPHY

"Arbeitsgesetz und Asylinitiative—Verunsicherung in Grenzen." *Neue Zürcher Zeitung*, December 3, 1996.

Auer, Andreas. *Le référendum et l'initiatives populaire aux Etats-Unis.* Basle: Helbing and Lichtenhahn, 1989.

Baschek, Eckhard. "Drogenmarkt Schweiz: Das Milliardengeschäft mit dem Rauschgift." *Schweizerische Handels-Zeitung,* November 16, 1995, p. 3.

Bernegger, Michael. "Die Schweiz und die Weltwirtschaft: Abschied vom 'Sonderfall'?" In *Sonderfall? Die Schweiz zwischen Réduit und Europa: Ausstellung im Schweizerischen Landesmuseum Zürich, 19. August bis 15. November 1992,* eds. Watler Leimgruber and Gabriela Christen. Zurich: Schweizerisches Landesmuseum, 1992, pp. 59–79.

Borner, Silvio; Aymo Brunetti; and Thomas Straubhaar. *Schweiz AG. Vom Sonderfall zum Sanierungsfall?* Zurich: Verlag Neue Zürcher Zeitung, 1990.

Bretscher-Spindler, Katharina. "Im Spannungsfeld von Familie und Beruf. Notwendiges Überdenken der Geschlechterrollen von Mann und Frau." *Neue Zürcher Zeitung,* April 16, 1994, p. 75.

Brüderl, Josef; Andreas Diekmann; and Henriette Engelhardt. "Einkommensunterschiede zwischen Frauen und Männern in der Schweiz. Eine Zerlegung des Einkommensabstands mit der Komponentenmethode." *Swiss Journal of Sociology* 19 (1993), pp. 573–588.

Buchmann, Marlis; M. Koenig; J. H. Li; and S. Sacchi. *Berufliche Aufstiegschancen und Abstiegsrisiken im Wandel.* Berne: Federal Office of Statistics, 1996.

Buhmann, Brigitte I. *Armut in der reichen Schweiz: eine verdrängte Wirklichkeit,* Zürich, Wiesbaden: Orell Füssli Verlag, 1989.

Bütschi, Danielle, and Sandro Cattacin. *Le modèle suisse du bien-être. Coopération conflictuelle entre Etat et societé civile: le cas de l'alcoolisme et du vih / sida.* Lausanne: Réalités sociales, 1994.

Camartin, Iso; C. Pier Conti; Doris Jakubec; and Peter von Matt. Die Literaturen der Schweiz: Analysen gemeinsamer Brennpunkte, Basle: Frankfurt, 1992, p.91

Charles, Maria, and Marlis Buchmann. "Assessing Micro-Level Explanations of Occupational Sex Segregation: Human-Capital Development and Labor Market Opportunities in Switzerland." *Swiss Journal of Sociology* 20, no. 3 (1994), pp. 595–620.

Clinton, Bill, "Strengthening Communities. Response to Drugs and Crime." Message from the President to the Congress of the United States, http://www.ncjrs-org/txtfiles/, 1996.

Coordinating Commission for the Presence of Switzerland Abroad [CCPSA], Federal Department for Foreign Affairs, in cooperation with the Arts Council of Switzerland Pro Helvetia, Switzerland. *Culture.* Berne, 1993.

Coordinating Commission for the Presence of Switzerland Abroad [CCPSA], Federal Department for Foreign Affairs, in cooperation with the Swiss Documentation Center for Education, Switzerland. *Education and Training.* Berne, 1993b.

Coordinating Commission for the Presence of Switzerland Abroad [CCPSA], Federal Department for Foreign Affairs, Switzerland. *Social Structure. An Information Sheet.* Berne, 1993c.

Daalder, Hans, ed., *Party Systems in Denmark, Austria, Switzerland, the Netherlands and Belgium.* London: Frances Printer, 1987.

Dunant, Henry. *A Memory of Solferino.* 1862. Reprint, Geneva: International Committee of the Red Cross, 1986.

"Economic Indicators." *The Economist,* December 13, 1997, p. 96.

"Eidgenössische Volksabstimmung. An einer asylpolitischen Blamage vorbei." December 2, 1996.

Erikson, Robert, and John H. Goldthorpe. *The Constant Flux: A Study of Class Mobility in Industrial Societies.* Oxford: Oxford University Press, 1993.

eurostat (ed.), *Begegnung in Zahlen. Ein statistisches Porträt der Schweiz im Europäischen Wirtschaftsraum.* Luxembourg: Amt für amtliche Veröffentlichungen der Europäischen Gemeinschaft, 1992.

"Farming." *The Economist,* June 1, 1996, p. 101.

Federal Chancellery. "Volksabstimmung vom 1. Dezember 1996. Erläuterungen des Bundesrates 1996."

Federal Commission for Women's Issues. *Great Achievements—Small Changes? On the Situation of Women in Switzerland.* Berne: Federal Commission for Women's Issues, 1995a.

Federal Office of Statistics. *Auf dem Wege zur Gleichstellung? Frauen und Männer in der Schweiz aus statistischer Sicht.* Berne: Federal Office of Statistics, 1993a.

Federal Office of Statistics. "Eidgenössische Volkszählung 1990, Neue Vielfalt der Sprachen und Konfessionen der Schweiz." Press Release No. 31/93, Berne, May 1993b.

Federal Office of Statistics. *Familien heute: Das Bild der Familie in der Volkszählung 1990.* Berne: Federal Office of Statistics, 1994a.

Federal Office of Statistics. *The 1990 Population Census: Switzerland in Profile.* Berne: Federal Office of Statistics, 1994b.

Federal Office of Statistics. *Bildungsindikatoren Schweiz. Bildungssystem(e) Schweiz im Wandel.* Berne: Federal Office of Statistics, 1995a.

Federal Office of Statistics. "Eidgenössische Volkszählung 1990: Ein Blick in die Sozialstruktur der Schweiz." Pressemitteilung No. 71/95, Berne, November 1995b.

Federal Office of Statistics. *Eidgenössische Volkszählung 1990—Die Bevölkerung der Schweiz—Struktur und räumliche Dynamik.* Berne: Federal Office of Statistics, 1995c.

Federal Office of Statistics. "Soziale Ungleichheit im Bildungswesen." Pressemitteilung No. 48/96, Berne, May 1996.

Federal Office of Statistics. "Die berufliche Flexibilität im Wandel." Pressemitteilung No. 4/96, Berne, 1996b.

Federal Office of Statistics. *Statistisches Jahrbuch der Schweiz 1996. Separatdruck Kapitel 1: Bevölkerung.* Zurich: Verlag Neue Zürcher Zeitung, 1996c.

Fleiner-Gerster, Thomas, and Kurt Lüscher, *Familien in der Schweiz.* Freiburg Universitätsverlag, 1991.

Frauchiger, Urs. *Entwurf Schweiz. Anstiftung zur kulturellen Rauflust.* Zurich: Ammann, 1995.

Füglistaler-Wasmer, Peter. *Sozialpolitische Massnahmen im Kampf gegen die Armut in der Schweiz.* Berne, Stuttgart, Wien: P. Haupt Verlag, 1992.

Hainard, François; Marion Nolde; Gilberte Memminger; and M. Micheloni. *Avons-nous des pauvres? Enquête sur la précarité et la pauvreté dans le canton de Neuchâtel.* Neuchâtel: Université de Neuchâtel, 1990.

Hasler, Eveline. *Flying with Wings of Wax: The Story of Emily Kempin-Spyri.* Translated by Edna McCown. New York: Fromm International, 1994.

Haug, Werner. *Vom Einwanderungsland zur multikulturellen Migrationspolitik. Grundlagen für eine schweizerische Migrationspolitik.* Berne: Federal Office of Statistics, 1995.

Hilowitz, Janet Eve, ed., *Switzerland in Perspective.* New York: Greenwood Press, 1990.

Hoffmann-Nowotny, Hans-Joachim. "Analytisch alter Wein in ideologisch neuen Schläuchen." Zurich *Unizürich,* February 1996, pp. 6–9.

Höltschi, Peter, and Alberto Venzago. "Migros, Marta, Mövenpick." *GEO Special Schweiz,* November 11, 1987, pp. 104–114.

Horowitz, Irving Lewis. *C. Wright Mills: An American Utopian.* New York: Free Press, 1983.

Hotz, Beat. *Politik zwischen Staat und Wirtschaft.* Dissenhofen: Rüegger, 1979.

Hotz-Hart, Beat; Stefan Maeder; and Patrick Vock. *Volkswirtschaft der Schweiz.* Zurich: vdf Hochschulverlag AG an der ETH Zürich, 1995.

Im Hof, Ulrich. *Geschichte der Schweiz und der Schweizer.* Basle and Frankfurt a.M.: Helbing & Lichtenhahn, 1986.

Katzenstein, Peter J. *Small States in World Markets.* Ithaca, NY: Cornell University Press, 1985.

Kearl, M., "Kearl's Guide to the Sociology of the Family." http://WWW.Trinity.Edu/~mkearl, Trinity University, 1996.

Kellerhals, Jean M., and Josette Coenen-Huther. "Some Aspects of the Structure and Functioning of the Family in Switzerland." In *Switzerland in Perspective,* ed. Janet Eve Hilowitz. New York: Greenwood Press, 1990, pp. 117–35.

Kerbo, Harold K., *Social Stratification and Inequality: Class Conflict in Historical and Comparative Perspecive,* 3d ed., New York: McGraw-Hill, 1996.

Kerr, Henry H. *Parlement et société en Suisse.* Saint-Saphorin: Georg, 1981.

Kerr, Henry H. "The Swiss Party System: Steadfast and Changing." In *Party Systems in Denmark, Austria, Switzerland, the Netherlands and Belgium,* ed. Hans Daalder. London: Frances Printer, 1987, pp. 107–92.

Kreis, Georg. *Die Schweiz unterwegs: Schlussbericht des NFP 21 "Kulturelle Vielfalt und Identität."* Basel: Frankfurt a.M., Helbing & Lichtenhahn, 1993.

Kriesi, Hanspeter. *Entscheidungsstrukturen und Entscheidungsprozesse in der Schweizer Politik.* Frankfurt, Campus, 1980.

Kriesi, Hanspeter. *Le Système Politique Suisse.* Paris: Ed. Economica, 1995.

Kriesi, Hanspeter, R. Koopmans, J. W. Duyvendak, and M. Giugni. *The Politics of New Social Movements in Western Europe. A Comparative Analysis.* Minneapolis: University of Minnesota Press, 1995a.

Kriesi, Hanspeter; Claude Longchamps; Florence Passy; Pascal Sciarini, *Analysi della votazione federale del 6 dicembre 1992. VOX Analisi di votazioni federali: Proposta federale sullo Spazio Economico Europeo.* Pubblicazione no. 47 Adliswil and Geneva: GfS Istituto di ricera and Università di Ginevra, 1993, pp. 64.

Kriesi, Hanspeter; Boris Wernli; Pascal Sciarini; and Matteo Gianni. "Le clivage linguistique: problèmes de compréhension entre les communautés linguistiques en Suisse," Deptartment of Political Science, University of Geneva, 1995b.

Lassueur, Yves, and Sabine Pirolt. "Le vrai visage de la pauvreté en Suisse." *L'Hebdo*, March 21, 1996.

Lechner-Bovey, Madeleine; Graf, Martin; Hotz-Huber, Annemarie, eds., *Le Parlement*—"Autorité Suprême de la Confédération?" Berne: Haupt, 1991.

Leimgruber, Walter, and Gabriela Christen, eds. *Sonderfall? Die Schweiz zwischen Réduit und Europa: Ausstellung im Schweizerischen Landesmuseum Zürich, 19. August bis 15. November 1992*. Zurich: Schweizerisches Landesmuseum, 1992.

Levy, René; Dominique Joye; Olivier Guye; and Vincent Kaufmann. Will be published as: *Tous égaux? De la stratification aux représentations*. Zurich: Seismo, 1997, forthcoming. Page numbers refer to unpublished manuscript.

Linder, Wolf. *Swiss Democracy. Possible Solutions to Conflict in Multicultural Societies*. New York: St. Martin's Press, 1994.

Lipset, Seymour M. *American Exceptionalism: A Double-Edged Sword*. New York: W. W. Norton, 1996.

Lipset, Seymour M., ed. *Consensus and Conflict. Essays in Political Sociology*. New Brunswick, NJ: Transaction Books, 1985.

Lipset, Seymour M., and Stein Rokkan. "Cleavage Structures, Party Systems, and Voter Alignments." In *Consensus and Conflict. Essays in Political Sociology*, ed. Seymour M. Lipset. New Brunswick, NJ, Transaction Books, 1985, pp. 113–85.

Lüscher, Kurt, and Rüdiger Thierbach. "Die demographische Vielfalt des Alleinlebens. Einpersonenhaushalte in der Volkszählung 1990." *Neue Zürcher Zeitung*, March 8, 1994, p. 23.

Margelisch, Hedi. Director, Business House. Interview, St. Gallen, August 27, 1996.

Melich, Anna, ed. *Les valeurs des Suisses*. Berne: Peter Lang S. A., 1991.

Mills, C. Wright. *The Power Elite*. New York: Oxford University Press, 1956.

Organization for Economic Co-operation and Development [OECD]. *Reviews of National Policies for Education: Switzerland*. Paris: OECD, 1991.

Poitry, Alain-Valéry. *La fonction d'ordre de l'Etat. Analyse des mécanismes et des déterminants sélectifs dans le processus législatif suisse*. Berne: Lang, 1989.

Ragin, Charles, and David Zaret. "Theory and Method in Comparative Strategies" *Social Forces* 61 (1983), pp. 731–54.

Riklin, Alois, Silvano Möckli. "Milizparlament?" In *Le Parlement— "Autorité Suprême de la Confédération"?*, ed. M. Bovey-Lechner et al. Berne: Haupt, 1991, pp. 145–63.

Rodger, Ian. "Manufacturing: Feeling the Pinch." *Financial Times (London)*, April 15, 1996, p. IV.

Schaefer, Richard T., and Robert P. Lamm. *Sociology*. New York: McGraw-Hill, 1989.

Schuler, Martin, and Dominique Joye. "Die räumliche Dynamik in der Schweiz: Tendenzen zwischen zwei Volkszählungsjahren," pp. 111–74, in *Eidgenössische Volkszählung 1990—Die Bevölkerung der Schweiz—Struktur und räumliche Dynamik* (Berne: Federal Office of Statistics, 1995).

Smelser, Neil J. *Comparative Methods in the Social Sciences*. Englewood Cliffs, NJ: Prentice Hall, 1976.

Sorg, Eugen. "Zürich Sucht." *Tages-Anzeiger Magazin*, December 3, 1994, pp. 8–63.

Spillmann, Kurt R., Rolf Kieser, Blickpunkt Schweiz, Zurich, Verlag Neue Zürcher Zeitung, 1995.

Suter, Christian; Monica Budowski; and Peter C. Meyer, *Einkommensschwäche, Untervetsorgung und Mangellagen bei alleinerziehenden Müttern in der Stadt Zürich: Ergebnisse einer Längsschnittstudie,* Swiss Journal of Sociology: 22/1, 1996, pp. 27–57.

"The Discrete Charm of the Multicultural Multinational." *The Economist,* June 30, 1994, pp. 59–60.

"The Family. Home Sweet Home." *The Economist,* September 9, 1995, pp. 25–26.

"The Great Debate." Surrey. *The Economist,* September 21, 1996.

Vatter, Adrian. "Der EWR-Entscheid: Kulturelle Identität, rationales Kalkül oder struktureller Kontext?" *Swiss Journal of Sociology* 20, no. 1 (1994); pp. 14–42.

Western, Mark, and Erik Olin Wright. "The Permeability of Class Boundaries to Intergenerational Mobility among Men in the United States, Canada, Norway and Sweden." *American Sociological Review* 59 (August 1994), pp. 606–29.

"Where to Live: Nirvana by Numbers." *The Economist,* December 25, 1993–January 7, 1994, pp. 73–76.

Zanoni, Urs. *Die Stadionen der Vertreiburg,* Zurich: Die Weltwoche, September 1994, p. 33.

There are relatively few English language Web sites on Switzerland. Often it is more productive to do a search using "Switzerland" in combination with other relevant key terms. Here are some sites with interesting links and material:

http://www.keele.ac.uk/depts/po/area/switzerl.htm

Keele University in Great Britain operates an area studies program on the Web. This is the URL for the Switzerland page.

http://kuznets.fas.harvard.edu/~sfeldman/swiss.html

Sven Feldmann's site provides many links to Swiss institutions, political issues, and sites of cultural interest.

http://www.yahoo.com/Regional/Countries/Switzerland/

This brings up a field for Yahoo keyword searches on Switzerland.

http://www.admin.ch/

The Federal Authorities of the Swiss Confederation.

http://www.swissembassy.org.uk/

The Swiss Embassy to the United Kingdom has even more English language material.

http://www-scf.usc.edu/~sschmidt/swiss.html

Scott Schmidt's homepage devoted solely to Swiss foreign policy.

http://www.eda-tf.ethz.ch/homef_e.htm

Switzerland in the Second World War.

http://www.tages-anzeiger.ch/

http://www.nzz.ch/

For those who read German, the *Tages-Anzeiger* and the *Neue Zürcher Zeitung*, Zurich-based dailies, offer select articles.

http://www.webdo.ch/

Webdo—Presse suisse. A gateway to Swiss news in French.

agglomeration See **urbanization, cities.**

Alemannic Switzerland The German-speaking part of Switzerland; **Alemannic dialects:** dialects of German spoken in Switzerland, Alsace, and parts of southern Germany; **Alemanni:** German tribe that settled in those areas in the early Middle Ages.

Alps, Alpine mountains, transalpine tunnels A mountain system in central Europe, some 500 miles long and 100 miles wide. It covers parts of France, Italy, Switzerland, Liechtenstein, Germany, Austria, and Slovenia, but the countries with the strongest Alpine presence are Switzerland and Austria. The Mont Blanc, on the French–Italian border, is the highest Alpine mountain (15,771 ft). The highest peak in Switzerland is the Monte Rosa (15,203 ft), on the border with Italy. Some 60 percent of the Swiss territory is covered by the Alpine region, including hilly country. The Alps are pierced by a number of railroad and automobile tunnels, of which the Saint Gotthard (9 miles/15 km long) and Simplon (12 miles/19 km long) are the longest.

ascribed status, ascriptive factors A status that is assigned to the individual at birth or at different stages of the life cycle; forces that translate ascribed status into some social consequence. The opposite is achieved status, a social position that an individual earns through his and her own effort.

bicameralism A legislative system composed of two chambers, such as Senate and House of Representatives in the United States, and **Council of States** and **National Council** in Switzerland.

canton A French word for an administrative or political entity, generally at a lower level of government; in Switzerland the middle tier in the federalist government structure. Although by size more related to American counties, their history as sovereign states before 1848 as well as fully-fledged organs of government make the Swiss cantons akin to the states of the United States. There are 23 cantons: 20 full cantons and 6 half-cantons, a status that determines representation in the federal parliament. A table of **cantonal** areas and population is found in chapter 1.

capitalism An economic system based on the principles of private ownership, the profit motive, and free competition; adj. **capitalist** (economy), **capitalistic** (behavior). In Switzerland, the term more often used for capitalism is "free market economy."

cartel A combination of independent business organizations formed to regulate production, pricing, and marketing of goods by the members; **cartellization,** the act of forming a cartel; the degree to which businesses in a sector are bound by cartel rules.

centrality The position in the middle or center of something, a key position in a network of relationships. The opposite is a position at the **periphery.**

church A religious organization with wide acceptance as legitimate, and with values and practices that are seen as the normal way to practice religion in a given society.

cities Major cities are Zurich (German spelling: Zürich; population in 1994: 343,000), Genèva (French spelling: Genève; 172,000), Berne (Bern; 129,000), Basle (Basel; 176,000), Lausanne (117,000). Berne is the federal capital. All cities form part of urban agglomerations whose total population is much larger than the municipal figures shown here.

commune The lowest-level political subdivision, comparable to the American town and city, governed by a commune or municipal council. There are some 3,000 communes in Switzerland. The communes cover the entire national territory; there are no unincorporated areas. The next higher political tier is the canton (see **cantons**); districts have administrative and judicial functions between communes and cantons. Besides the political communes, church, school, and burger communes exist, the latter vested with powers to naturalize foreigners.

communitarian Lifestyles and social philosophies that emphasize a person's duties toward his or her community, and the community's responsibility to look after the welfare of its members, as opposed to individualistic beliefs that stress the freedom and self-responsibility of the individual.

Confederation The federal level of government, but also, as Swiss Confederation, the official name of the country. Originally a confederation of small sovereign states, the present-day cantons, the modern federal state, founded in 1848, expresses its far-reaching division of power between center and cantons through this term. The adjective, however, is **"federal,"** the power-sharing aspect of government is **"federalism,"** and the resemblance with the confederates of the American Civil War is purely accidental.

conservative See **liberal.**

cosmopolitan Literally, a citizen of the world; somebody so sophisticated as to be at home in all parts of the world or conversant with many spheres of interest. Here it is used to characterize persons and groups in Switzerland with an open, aggressive outlook to the international and intercultural environment. The opposite in this context is **traditionalist.** The cosmopolitan–traditionalist polarity in Swiss cultural and political life has been added to the earlier exclusively **left–right** orientation.

Council of States One of the chambers of the **Federal Assembly.** The citizens of each canton elect two State Councilors, those of a half-canton one, for a total of 46 Councilors.

culture The sum of symbols used by a society, notably its language, but also including rules for behavior called *norms*, as well as beliefs and values. Culture can be most broadly understood as the blueprint a society has for living.

democracy Government by the people (from Greek *demos*, meaning people), either by their direct decision making (direct democracy) or through elected representatives (representative democracy).

direct democracy See **democracy.**

European Economic Area *See European Union.*

European Union   Formerly the European Community, the supranational organization formed in 1967 by a merger of specialized central European collaborative organizations. With 12 member states—Belgium, Denmark, France, Germany, Greece, Ireland, Italy, Luxembourg, the Netherlands, Portugal, Spain, and the United Kingdom—until 1991. The Union has since been in a process of enlargement the end of which is difficult to foresee. Since 1993 there have been no restrictions on the movement of goods, services, capital, workers, and tourists within the Union, on the way to an integrated **European Economic Area** (EEA). The EU headquarters is in Brussels, Belgium. The Swiss people rejected joining the EEA in December 1992.

factor endowment   An economy's supply with the things ("production factors") necessary to produce and to trade, such as land, mineral resources, industrial plant, skills, and capital, and the relative prices at which those various factors are available.

Federal Assembly   The combined two chambers of the Swiss parliament. It brings together the **National Council,** comparable to the House of Representatives in the United States, and the **Council of States,** comparable to the Senate.

Federal Council   The seven-person executive body of the federal government, elected by the **Federal Assembly** for a four-year term. The Council is led by the **president of the Confederation.** He/she, however, does not hold executive powers like the American president. The presidency rotates annually.

federalism   See **Confederation.**

fiscal   Pertaining to government expenditures, revenues, and debt.

French Revolution   Massive upheaval in France that started in 1789 and led to the destruction of the medieval social order as well as to wars that engulfed most of Europe, including Switzerland.

gender   The social characteristics that a society considers proper for its males and females; the attitudes and activities linked to each sex.

German-speaking Switzerland   The part of Switzerland where **Swiss-German,** a collection of German dialects, is spoken. Also called **Alemannic Switzerland.**

Germanic languages, countries   A group of languages to which, inter alia, German, Dutch and English belong. Germanic countries may refer more exclusively to the mostly German-speaking countries of Germany, Austria, Switzerland, and Liechtenstein.

globalization   The process of making something worldwide in scope or application, such as financial markets and manufacturing arrangements.

government quota   The share of government consumption and government transfer payments (e.g. social security) in the national income.

Gymnasium   See *Maturität.*

Helvetians, or Helvetii   A Celtic tribe occupying large parts of modern Switzerland in pre-Christian times, subjected by the Romans in 58 BC. The Latin name for Switzerland is Confoederatio Helvetica, and **Helvetia** is a frequent poetic and mystical reference to the country, such as in **Mother Helvetia.**

immigrants, immigration Persons who leave, the process of leaving, one country in order to settle in another. In Switzerland, the term used for the immigrant population is "foreigners" (German: *Ausländer,* French: *les étrangers*), rarely immigrants or aliens. While immigration to Switzerland in the 20th century is an important phenomenon, emigration has played a minimal role in this period.

initiative A procedure by which citizens can force parliaments to consider an amendment to the federal constitution or a law or measure at the lower tiers or, if the concerned parliament does not adopt the proposition, a popular ballot. Federal constitutional initiatives require the signatures of 100,000 citizens.

institution Problem-solving grouping in society, such as the family, organized around stable sets of norms, values, and roles.

integrated, integration See **social integration.**

interdenominational Involving several denominations, often referring to spouses raised in different faiths.

Jura The third of the major Swiss landscape formations, besides the **Alps** and the **Midlands,** a chain of hills and low mountains extending along the French–Swiss and Swiss–German borders and rising to 5,652 ft. It covers about 10 percent of the national surface.

latent function The unintended and often unrecognized function of a behavior pattern or social arrangement. The opposite term is **manifest function.**

left, right Named after the seating arrangement in one of the conventions during the French Revolution, left in the political and intellectual arenas has come to denote political parties and individuals of **socialist** conviction, whereas the right includes their **conservative,** pro-capitalist opposites. Forces holding a middle position between left and right are called the political center.

liberal, conservative These terms carry different meanings in the United States and Switzerland. While US liberals are often seen to be cultural liberals and politically left-leaning (with conservatives as their opposites), the Swiss liberals go back to urban, Protestant, pro-capitalist milieux. They are thus part of the conservative side of party politics, although mostly with a more open mind on Switzerland's greater participation in European affairs than other conservatives. The antonym of conservative in Swiss politics is **socialist.** In the economy, liberal denotes freedom from government controls.

manifest function The intended and recognized function of a behavior or social arrangement. The opposite term is **latent function.**

market niche A special area of demand for a product or service, which then may be met through the economic activity specially suited to the interests, abilities, and factor endowments of an individual, firm, or country.

Maturität (German; French: *maturité*) Swiss high school **(Gymnasium)** leaving certificate usually taken at age 19, good for university admission. *Maturitätsschulen:* schools that bestow that degree.

Midlands Also called the **Central Plateau.** The densely populated, gently undulating swathe of land that stretches between Lake Geneva in the west and

Lake Constance in the northeast, bounded by the Alps in the south and the Jura in the northwest. Except for Basle, all major cities form part of the Midlands.

monopoly   Exclusive possession or control, particularly over a commodity, service, or area of expertise. An organization wielding such control.

Mother Helvetia   See **Helvetians.**

multiculturalism   A society characterized by close interaction between different cultures; sometimes used normatively as a positive value attached to cultural diversity and as a duty to respect cultural differences. Adj. **multicultural.** See also **multilingual.**

multilingual   Societies, groups, or institutions in which several languages are used side by side. Also, a person speaking several languages.

Muslim   A believer of Islam.

myth   A traditional, typically ancient story dealing with supernatural beings, ancestors, or heroes that serves as a fundamental type in the world view of a people, by explaining aspects of the natural world or delineating the psychology, customs, or ideals of society.

National Council   Its 200 members are elected in proportion to party-list votes cast within each of the cantons or semi-cantons.

Nazism, Nazi era   The rule of National Socialism, or Nazism, in Germany under Adolf Hitler, 1933–45, who led Europe into World War II, committed the Holocaust and other genocide, and was defeated by an alliance of Western powers and the Soviet Union. This period is part of the fascist era, so called after the right-wing régimes in Italy and Spain. Switzerland was surrounded by the fascist powers of Germany and Italy from 1940 to 1944.

neutrality   A state or policy of being neutral, especially nonparticipation in war.

nuclear family   A mother and/or father, and their unmarried children forming an independent household. A family that includes other kin as well is called extended family.

per capita income   National income of a given year divided by population size; thus average income per person.

peripheral   Adj. of **periphery,** the outermost part of a region. See **centrality.**

pragmatism   A value system geared to practical results, concerned with facts, and ready to make compromises in the interest of success. Adj. **pragmatic.** The opposite is *dogmatism, dogmatic,* the determination to stick to one's tenets of faith or a laid-down doctrine at the cost of achieving practical results.

preparliamentary   That part of a law and budget making that takes place before parliament considers it. Mostly used in connection with the extensive consultations that the Swiss system of government arranges between special interest groups, experts, administrators, and representatives at the early stages of a legislative project.

quasi-monopolistic   Enjoying a virtual monopoly. See *monopoly.*

referendum   Either a mandatory popular ballot on a constitutional amendment or international treaty, or a ballot that a minimum number of citizens demand on a law passed by a parliament. At the federal level, 50,000 signatures are required to force a referendum. Plural: **referenda,** or referendums. See also **initiative.**

Reformation   A 16th-century movement in Western Europe that aimed at reforming doctrines and practices of the Roman Catholic Church and resulted in the establishment of the Protestant churches and in prolonged religious wars.

right   See **left.**

Romandie   The French-speaking part of Switzerland. Adjective: **Romand.**

Romanic   Or Romance languages, a family of languages that includes, among others, French, Italian, Spanish, Portuguese, and Romansh. Closely related to Latin.

Romansh   One of the four national languages in Switzerland, besides German, French, and Italian.

social class   In one of the most general definitions, a grouping of individuals with similar positions and similar political and economic interests within the stratification system. Most sociological class theories broadly assume the coexistence of three classes—lower, middle and upper—with varying degrees of internal distinctions.

Social Democrats   See **socialist.**

social integration   The degree to which people feel part of social groups, or to which life together can be organized without conflict; in Switzerland often used with regard to the assimilation of foreigners into Swiss culture and institutions.

social mobility   Movement to a significant degree up or down within a system of social stratification. Social mobility is often divided into two types: intergenerational social mobility, movement up or down compared to one's parents, and intragenerational social mobility, movement up or down in one's own lifetime.

social movement   Efforts by a large number of people to produce social change, often organized in networks connecting full-time activists, occasional supporters, and sympathizers.

social problem   Situation and condition shared by a significant number of people and defined as negative or harmful in the society. What comes to be defined as such is strongly influenced by those who have more power or influence within the society.

social structure   The system of social positions that individuals hold in society and of the relations among them within groups and among groups or categories of people.

socialist   Refers to the communist and social-democratic parties of the political **left.** In Switzerland, the communists, who originally demanded collective ownership of the means of production, enjoyed little support after the Second World War. The Social Democrats, supporters of a strong welfare state, are part of the governing coalition.

special-interest group, special-interest association   An alliance, often for political lobbying, of people who share an interest in some economic or social issue.

stratification   Social stratification: The division of a society into groups (strata) along a hierarchical dimension.

traditionalist   See **cosmopolitan.**

transalpine   See **Alps.**

United Nations   International organization established immediately after World War II to maintain international peace and security and to achieve cooperation in solving international economic, social, cultural, and humanitarian problems. Its headquarters is in New York. Switzerland is not a member of the United Nations, but supports various of its special-purpose agencies financially.

urbanization   The process of growth of town and cities, sometimes into vast urban **agglomerations** or a metropolis. See also **cities.**

venture capital   Money made available for investment in innovative enterprises or research, especially in high technology, in which both the risk of loss and the potential for profit may be considerable.

Volksschule   Also *Primarschule:* primary school.

xenophobic   Fearful or contemptuous of that which is foreign, especially of strangers or foreigners; anti-immigrant.